Read November 1979.

Read September 2016.

STAND FAST, THE HOLY GHOST

This is the gloriously epicurean story of Rupert Grayson in the thirties. The scion of a rich and indulgent shipbuilding family, he was able to devote himself to a life of elegant but picaresque fun in the company of his friends and relations, the beautiful and the cosmopolitan, all over the world. His restlessness and curiosity took him at whim from London to Bucharest, from Paris to the Matopo Hills, at the same time writing thrillers, at least when his adventures en route allowed. But the all-pervading influence of his father, Sir Henry Grayson (known to his family as H.M.G.), brought him back to London to work in the newly-acquired family publishing house as an editorial scout. This apparently more stable life was entirely to his taste, affording him endless opportunities to meet and mix with the gifted and eccentric in his search for authors. Soon, however, he was travelling again, this time to Hollywood with his twin brothers. Nine months later he returned, having made a film of Hollywood and its stars. But the War broke out, forcing Grayson & Grayson to close down; the book leaves him proceeding to the Admiralty—to take an oath on the Official Secrets Act.

By the same author

FICTION

Scarlet Livery
Gun Cotton
Death Rides the Forest
Gun Cotton—Adventurer
Escape with Gun Cotton
Gun Cotton in Hollywood
Gun Cotton—Secret Agent
Murder at the Bank
Introducing Mr Robinson
Adventure Nine
Blind Man's Hood
Ace High
Gun Cotton in Mexico
Secret Airman
Outside the Law
Gun Cotton Goes to Russia

AUTOBIOGRAPHY

Voyage Not Completed

STAND FAST, THE HOLY GHOST

RUPERT GRAYSON

Tom Stacey

First published in London in 1973
by Tom Stacey Ltd.
28-29 Maiden Lane, London WC2E 7JP

ISBN 0 85468 452 2

Printed in Great Britain by
Clarke, Doble & Brendon Ltd.
Plymouth

LIST OF ILLUSTRATIONS

In gratitude and affection
to
Felix and Kikki Rankin
at whose home this weary traveller
has so often found rest

Author's note : Had I been in the Royal Navy my favourite bugle blast would certainly have been the age-old call, 'Up spirits!' Alas, the rum ration has been discontinued, so no longer will the old sailor mumble into his beard, 'Stand fast, the Holy Ghost!'

CHAPTER I

Safe home, safe home again in port
Cordage rent, shatter'd deck
Torn sails, provisions short
And only not a wreck.

HYMNS OF THE EASTERN CHURCH

I braced myself to die, pulling tightly on my seat belt and wedging my diplomatic bags around me for protection. The money I owed the Foreign Office had suddenly become a matter of no importance. We had taken off from Piaco airport, Trinidad, climbing into a dawn sky. I occupied the usual two seats reserved for the King's Messenger—myself. My account with my masters (the Foreign Office) was £300 in the red so I had passed my time trying to bring my expense-sheets into harmony with the situation: arithmetic was never my strong point.

On the miserable allowance the F.O. doled out, unless a messenger was prepared to cut out the necessities of life—fine linen, good food and wine, grand opera and lovely women of all nationalities—it was impossible for him to lead a civilized existence without monies of his own inheritance. Thus, when it happened, my mind was occupied with calculations foreign to my nature. The starboard engine stuttered, coughed and cut out. Our air hostess, with whom I had flown many times, had already been called to the cockpit, and now she reappeared, a fixed smile on her young face: it had become necessary, she announced, to make an emergency landing; would we therefore please make sure our seat belts were fastened.

We had begun our descent into the swirling eiderdown of cloud that had already blotted out the voracious Brazilian jungle lying in wait for us. In six months' time there would be little trace of either plane fabric or passenger flesh after plants and insects had gorged their fill on us. I had been flying this route now, usually at about 10,000 feet, twice a month for two years—it was before the days of pressurized cabins—and I had often marvelled at the seething green of the jungle stretching below us to every compass point at the rim of the world. It was an area of the earth's surface more cruel than the sea, more secret than the mountains and more merciless than the desert.

I knew that there were occasional strips in the jungle cleared for such an emergency as this, but in these immensities the chance of finding one was one in a million against. Fear began to communicate itself from one to the other. Even the children seemed to sense danger. That unmistakable yet indescribable smell of fear had already seeped into the cabin, the hearing had become correspondingly acute, and there was the low chanting and the click of beads and the whisper of Aves and Paters. Above it I heard the more prosaic sound of hard breathing, dry coughs, the nervous shuffling of feet; the air was gradually being saturated with the stench of vomit and emptying bowels. In the mounting fear I seemed to smell the sangria of blood and excrement that rises from a bullring when the animals (men, horses, bull) first sense the imminence of death.

The young air hostess moved amongst us like a technological Florence Nightingale: as she passed my seat and checked my seat belt I felt her trembling hand flutter on my wrist as if to recharge the batteries of her own courage. She must have felt no reaction from me; for I had long hoped that when death came it would strike after the manner of a Viking rite, fire devouring the cabin and flaring across the wings, so that in this pagan consummation an all-seeing God would recognize the burning cross of His own sacrifice and our salvation.

The wind wailed and thrust us downwards as if determined to join in the work of destruction by nailing us to the magnetic earth, helpless, sightless and coffined.

Suddenly we broke cloud. Directly ahead lay the miracle. An

emergency landing strip stretched like a beautiful green and brown carpet; or can I say, extravagantly, like an altar cloth, for it must have been God Himself who had spread it for our safety.

As we jolted to a landing, instead of relief and cries of joy a sighing stillness fell on us; resigned to death we were stunned into silence by the realization we were still alive.

The pilot came out from the cockpit, a smile of infinite tenderness on his sweating face. He had flown us through the shadow of death; we were his children and he loved us, but I could feel the tremor of his hand as he gripped the back of my seat.

The plane was quickly cleared and the passengers split into groups discussing the adventure and our escape. I wandered to the edge of the clearing, where the forest twilight deepened into distant and impenetrable green.

Alone with my thoughts and prayers I was surprised by the sudden appearance of a ragged, bearded figure. Without speaking he spread a cloth at my feet, piled with rough uncut aquamarines and sapphires. At the same moment I heard the co-pilot summoning me back by name; for he had promised not to allow anyone on the plane before the King's Messenger. Quickly I gave the man a fistful of notes and coins; he must have been satisfied because he poured the gems into my cupped hands.

The fuel blockage, the instrument of death, or whatever it was, had been repaired and we took off again, landing in Rio without further trouble. Here I was met by the ambassadorial car. I delivered my green-striped diplomatic bags at the Embassy; and was then driven to the Hotel Gloria. Later, with the help of my old friend the hall porter I sold the stones for a sum far exceeding the amount due to the Foreign Office.

Once again I had been saved by the gong. Someone had once said of me that if I chose to throw myself into the River Thames I would be washed up in the Savoy Grill. It wasn't as if I lived dangerously or even romantically, but I seemed always to be balanced on the edge of crisis, and as a result always in the process of extricating myself from my self-inflicted follies.

Many years before all this, seeking to escape from the shock of a broken marriage, and the aimlessness of a pleasure-seeking life in the jazz-age of the Roaring Twenties, I had shipped as deck-hand in bug-ridden tramps trading in the Caribbean and South American gulf ports.

A man had died violently. I, although innocent, had been held in some suspicion: and came to be looked on as a Jonah by my superstitious shipmates.

When we sailed into New York on Christmas Eve I had jumped the ship. I was without passport or identification papers, a deserter in maritime law and a criminal in the eyes of the authorities. I had only escaped the police through the help of an Irish jarvey who knew every twist and corner of the murky 'underground' that operates in New York, as in all great ports. Paddy had slipped me through the meshes of the law and I now was on my way back to England, heart heavy, because I knew only too well my Seaman's Discharge Book would be defaced for all time with the dread words 'Voyage Not Completed', epitaph of my career as a seaman.

All my efforts to break away from the rich and conventional world into which I had luckily been born had proved a failure. It is said that all successes and disasters are grouped in threes. So far I had failed as a soldier, sailor and husband. But it was now clear that on my return to England I had to find a job.

Work with regular hours had no appeal. A life of strap-hanging as a commuter between home and office would have been a slow spiritual death and a complete surrender of the principles on which I was trying to conduct my life. Whatever employment I could get must be work that would interest; for I refused to believe in working for work's sake. I even expected it to be amusing.

Musing on this subject I realized that anything in which I was interested had not the remotest possibility of earning me a living. Moreover a rather aggravating doubt kept intruding. Was I, in my late twenties, in any way employable?

I had, for instance, an interest in mountain climbing. I had read books on the subject, the ascent of Everest, climbing in the Urals, the Andes, the Canadian Rockies and the New Zealand McKenzies. Through a telescope from the bar of the Grand Hotel in Zermatt I had watched intrepid Britons crawling up well-worn routes to the summit of the Matterhorn and had felt proud of my countrymen.

But as one who has suffered vertigo on the Snowdon mountain

railway, it could only be imagination or nightmare that would hoist me to that dangerous overhang on the Dents du Midi or drive pitons into the north face of the Eiger.

Then there was fishing, which held a strange fascination for me. I have watched anglers watching silent fish while I watched the wild life of the riverbank or lochside, seated on my shooting stick beside a luncheon basket of cooled Chablis, smoked salmon, game pie and a box of Larrañaga Coronas to keep away the midges. But there seemed little future for me as a fisherman; anyway, I'd never held a rod in my life. I was essentially a watcher, albeit a first-class watcher.

I might of course try for a job in an hotel: sartorially I was excellently rigged out to be a head waiter; I knew how a restaurant should be 'dressed', how to escort the prettiest women to the most prominent tables. I had quite a good smattering of wine mumbo-jumbo and could certainly pass muster as a *sommelier*, having made many enthusiastic excursions among the first-, second-, and even third-growth wines. Both these jobs called for a good memory (people, like wines, like their names to be remembered) but, with Wilde, I could remember names but unfortunately never faces. To overcome this, cloakroom attendants similarly afflicted will often attach a description rather than hand a regular customer a ticket. One night at the Savoy I grabbed my silk hat from its shelf and read on the slip inserted in the band, 'Guardsman type, sapphire-diamond front stud, tipsy'.

At last I remembered I was a director of *The World*, a weekly periodical in which my father was the principal shareholder. The editor was a strange chameleon-like character called West de Wend Fenton. Like Teddy Preston of the *Sunday Referee* at a later period, he wrote practically the entire issue himself, politics, foreign affairs, social occasions, astrology, cookery and racing—the only part of the paper he didn't write was the advertisements, and he'd have done these had there been a fee. He lived in St James's Street where he dispensed largesse; but his hospitality ceased when it came to finding space for the brilliant pieces I had bombarded him with. The nominal salary as a director plus a weekly luncheon at the Carlton Grill was not likely to set me on the road to journalistic fame and fortune.

In my dreams there was one job I'd have liked (if it existed)—

but who of my friends would recommend me as a courier-cum-tutor to the travelling son of a South American millionaire with a family of beautiful dark-eyed Chileñas, swathed in chinchillas?

The truth was that I had dedicated myself unselfishly and wholeheartedly to extracting as much pleasure from life as it had to offer. This included a vast amount of reading; the company of books I found almost as entertaining as that of women and, in most cases, far more rewarding. So, subconsciously, I knew the well-known finger of fate was pointing me to the great pursuit of writing. It was really for this that I had travelled the world and gone to sea: to learn how the others lived. I had looked into the bright eyes of danger and there were stories in me ready to be told. The spark was there, could I but fan it into flame.

I had gathered unforgettable recipes. Now was the time to try them out: the fire was burning bright on the hearth, the golden eggs were ready for the omelette, the wine glowed red and sparkled in the decanter. What more could a would-be writer aged 26 hope for, except the courage and the industry to go about his solitary task?

The trouble was I had no certainty of selling the stuff, and even were I successful it would be a long time before my earnings therefrom, as the lawyers say, would meet my expenditure. I might have lived within my income had I been a perfectionist like Ernest Laing, our beloved family secretary. Like the true gourmet, he could be satisfied with a spoonful of caviare, a ripe peach and a glass of champagne, but for me it had to be the whole jar, a branch of the tree and the full bottle. Though I liked to think I appreciated quality, I certainly wanted it in quantity. I had often been reminded that little fish taste sweet; but I have always preferred the dry things, climate, toast, humour and champagne—the only exception being kisses, which must, of course, be sweeter than sweet wine.

It was an English New Year to which I returned; the winter roses were crystal with frost, and in the gardens and parks ice glazed the lakes and the fountains were silent. But at our country home, Ravenspoint, in Anglesey, it would be exhilarating to be back once more in the special world of the Graysons. My brother Tristram, later to become a colonel in my old regiment, the Irish Guards, met me in London and together we drove there for the annual Christmas gathering. I say Christmas, for although it was January the celebrations were still in full progress. Christmas with us lasted far longer than the space allotted in the calendar.

On our journey north we had to put up at an inn at Stoney Stratford (or was it Fenny Stratford?) that must have been old in Dickens' day. The hotel was full so we had to share a bedroom. Resigned to this, we settled our bill against an early start in order to reach Anglesey in daylight. Like most hotels in those days there was no central heating, and had there been it could never have even taken the chill off the lofty Victorian room. We decided to sleep fully dressed, but even so the cold by one o'clock was so intense that we might have been two arctic explorers who had lost their sleeping bags. Clearly we must have more blankets, but how to get them, there was the rub; all the pulling on the old bell rope (until it snapped off) was of no avail, even though we could hear a tolling somewhere in the frozen bowels of the establishment. We thought next of the carpet to cover us, but this, we discovered, was nailed to the floor. Just as the question of sheer survival reached a climax my eyes fell on the old velvet curtains that covered, rather inadequately, the twenty-foot-high windows. To take them down we had to lift the only available chair, a very heavy one, on to the dressing-table. Fortunately, Tristram, being exceptionally tall, was then able to reach into the shadows where the curtain rail merged with the ceiling.

Balanced on this dangerously insecure base (it had porcelain wheels) with limbs numbed and fingers frozen, he reached up and unhooked each fold in the curtains. From my position far below Tris became lost to view in a cloud of dust. When at long last the task was accomplished it was about four in the morning and we had less than two hours to rest under this repellent covering, but luckily I prefer dirt to cold. The only thing missing from the memory of that abysmal visit was the maid's face when she entered the room in the morning to see the windows naked and her curtains gone.

That night we were home in the warmth and welcome of Ravenspoint with the wind howling round the solid sprawling house and ripping itself to shreds against the headland.

The annual gathering of the Graysons was like the hosting of the gael, an assembly vast and boisterous. Apart from the various aunts and uncles and my own immediate family of five brothers and six sisters, a new crop of nephews and nieces, Peters, Jeremys,

Patricks, Victors, Janes, Jills and Jilly Fitzes, had been produced in my absence. I could hardly help noticing that their nannies weren't a patch for looks on the sturdy *Bretonnes* Mother had recruited for us when we were children.

After the loneliness of my life at sea, where I'd almost forgotten what I looked like, I seemed to have found myself in the midst of an endless game; games with my little nephews and nieces by day, and, when they were abed, games and charades that their elders delighted in. For these Mother had cupboards and trunks bursting with costumes of every kind, wigs, grease-paint and dressing-up clothes, together with an armoury of swords, cutlasses, daggers and pistols.

My brother Brian was by far the most talented entertainer in the family. He had the extraordinary gift of using meaningless words which somehow or other managed to make sense. He could preach a sermon crammed with every clerical cliché but void of all order or sequence; and alarmingly impressive.

At other times he would lecture on ornithology with his Harrovian contemporary to assist Harry Elliott, who imitated the bird cries, the most moving of which were the mating calls. With Tristram as his fellow passenger, they became two Welsh farmers in a train discussing in Welsh David Lloyd George; and on one occasion they had that great and devious man himself convulsed with laughter. My father was a High Tory and had a kind of natural dislike for the little Radical; but Lloyd George had no prejudices where wealthy titled men were concerned and delighted in the lovely women of whom Ravenspoint and the cottages on the estate had more than their fair share. Anyway, as High Sheriff of the county it was Father's duty to offer hospitality to the country's Prime Minister, no matter what his politics, and in matters of duty Father had an old-fashioned strictness.

In the midst of all this gay turmoil my mother was as usual busy twelve hours of the day attending meetings at the Women's Institute, buying presents for a hundred birthdays, matching materials for old aunts and 'thrashing out' (no other expression suffices) her accounts. This meant trying to balance a mysterious 'budget', a word she loved to use but whose meaning she never really understood.

These charming but futile conferences with her secretary, Ernest Laing, usually took place after luncheon. She would be seated in a very businesslike way with her black book on her knees and a freshly sharpened pencil poised above a closely written page. He would be standing with his back to the fire swaying slightly, in his Scholte suit, with a red carnation and striped waistcoat, holding a cup of *café au fine* in one hand and a cigar between the jewelled fingers of the other. It took all his tact, humour and patience, of which he was never short, to listen, explain and cautiously balance his way through the intricate and completely illogical arguments Mother would present to account for her extravagances.

This business was conducted in an atmosphere of *fougère royale* and rich Havana smoke which spread in blue spirals as he brought his cigar down like a conductor's baton whenever he wished to make a point. However, Mother did most of the talking, allowing Ernest only an occasional 'But, Lady Grayson'. Ernest had long ago made up his mind that all that was expected of him was to keep Mother's expenditure within some limits. He certainly knew she was supporting several charming but very poor relations; but then Ernest was never a match for her, particularly as she knew that he himself gambled on the horses and the stock market with lamentable results. In addition to dresses she never wore but which, nonetheless, kept arriving in a never-ending procession of delivery-vans, Mother would order consignments of the most expensive soaps, hand towels of the finest linen and bath towels of the most exhilarating textures. These were things she knew about; but her knowledge of pennies and shillings and weights and measures was non-existent.

She once answered a telephone call from Harrods who were enquiring whether an order for a 7lb. or an 8lb. leg of lamb was correct. 'We have guests,' she was overheard to say, 'so it must be a 78lb. leg.'

She had a remarkable way of overcoming all obstacles. My younger brothers, the twins, Ambrose and Godfrey, were very backward in their lessons, due to their ability to charm Miss Severs, their governess, into playing *écarté* instead of adding and subtracting or conjugating Latin verbs. They could never have passed the Common Entrance examination into any of the public schools, but Mother was determined to get them into Downside. She had never before met Father Trafford, its famous head-master, but this delightful man immediately fell under her spell.

As every Gregorian of that period knows, this six-footer was a formidable character, a headmaster who was all-powerful, and a priest all-understanding. Before Mother left Downside she had his promise to accept them, a decision he never publicly regretted.

When the grandchildren came into her life she never spoke down to them. She could meet children on level terms and thus they accepted her as an equal. Speaking to one of the grandchildren she was heard protesting, 'How dare you accuse me—I never said anything of the sort.' She seemed to mean something different and lovable to every one of us and all our friends.

My sisters' girl friends were all delightful, each in their different way. One would come across them unexpectedly at dinner, or seated beside one in a car driving to the cinema, reading in the long loggia overlooking the sea, or freshly arrived from Madam Bois's most fashionable finishing school in Paris, and smelling deliciously of the Rue de la Paix.

Father was not an easy man; he took a long time to make friends. As a family we were happy-go-lucky, and if we took life by the hand, he took it by the throat. Having inherited £1,000 a year at the age of 17 (in the days when money was money) he was quite independent of his parents. Thus, from an early age he was able to play host to his contemporaries, which probably had a lasting effect on his character; for though he was never really at home in his own house he was a difficult guest in anyone else's. In appearance he was remarkable. He stood six foot four and with his guardsman-like moustache and splendid bearing he looked like a military man. He had been intended for the army and had passed into the R.M.C., Sandhurst; but to his everlasting regret his father had asked him to take over the family shipbuilding firm, which he did from a sense of duty. When Tristram joined the Irish Guards as a regular officer, we all knew he could get away with murder where Father was concerned.

The newspapers invariably described him as the best-looking member of the House of Commons. He certainly attracted attention wherever he went and, like many shy men, though he assumed a stern look, he had a remarkably sweet smile which spread slowly across his perpetually brown face, for he tanned after a few minutes in the sun. I believe he was the only Member of Parliament who has ever been returned without making a single election speech. At the end of polling day when the votes had been counted and his majority of 10,000 announced, the loudest cry of approval came from a woman in the crowd who shouted, 'I wouldn't mind 'avin' a kid by you, mister.'

He befriended me even beyond the natural call of father to son because he recognized his own weaknesses in me. Before I had gone a-rovin' to the distant places on the earth he had made it clear he would no longer help me beyond the handsome allowance he already made me: for he was essentially a fair man and he was not prepared to continue doing for one of the family what he was not prepared to do for another. In short, he was ready to endure one, but one only, black sheep, and that sheep I knew only too well was marked for the shears. Almost hourly I waited for the summons to his room to be questioned as to my finances—my creditors, though very patient, were, alas, also very numerous—and cross-examined as to my future intentions.

But, although I didn't know it, time was working on my side. I once picked up a little leather book Mother had owned as a child. On the opening pages there were a number of questions. Question one: 'What is the most important thing in life?' In her schoolgirl copperplate she had written, 'To love and be loved'; and against the vague question, 'Who or what can be the greatest influence for good in your life?' (she was obviously meant to insert God, or the Catholic Church, or even prayer), she had written, 'Timing'.

Once more I was saved by the bell of destiny. Just as Taylor, his secretary, was advancing on me with the summons to Father's presence, the telephone rang. My old friend, Louis Drexel, married to my sister Nancy, was on the telephone inviting me to stay with them in the South of France where I could write to my heart's content, if not to that of my readers!

CHAPTER II

Marriage? All women should be married but no men.

KIERKEGAARD

Here all were noble, save Nobility.

BYRON

The next day I was in London. The family town house was all but closed. My marriage, like the Venetian tumbler that shattered when poison was poured into it, had ended, leaving me with a problem as complicated as the Polish corridor.

My wife Ruby (a cousin of Gertrude Lawrence) was living in Ennismore Street in her usual charmingly extravagant manner. She was one of the most beautiful women of her time; known in effigy from Land's End to John o'Groats, across the European and American continents and to the navies and armies of the world as 'The Kirchner Girl'. Kirchner, a Belgian artist (the Annigoni of his day) had used her as a model in a series of paintings whose reproductions spread like a rash or a vision of delight, according to your standpoint, throughout the universe. They decorated the walls of dugouts in France and Flanders and, for all I knew, every Eskimo igloo and African kraal.

At all periods in history, certain men, fortunate or unfortunate, win the love of a woman who already belongs to the masses. To women she represents a perfection denied them, to men she is the unattainable, the un-possible, uncompleted sex dream of frustrated longing. Even after our marriage Ruby remained 'The Kirchner Girl', recognized and fêted wherever she went. Her face appeared on picture postcards, the covers of *La Vie Parisienne*, calendars, playing cards and even Christmas greeting cards. I would be confronted suddenly in the Underground with her grey eyes looking into mine, as they were into the myriad strangers' eyes; a passing bus would whisk her smiling face beyond my vision. In my regiment, the Irish Guards, when I visited the Sergeants' or the Corporals' Mess with my younger brother Tristram, then a newly joined ensign, from the walls she would be watching me. Once, accompanying my brother on a barrack-room inspection, I saw the sergeant major's eyes flash, like a bayonet making a full point, at the guardsman standing to attention beside his cot. Pinned like a beautiful butterfly to the crucifix above his pillow was a pin-up of my wife, 'The Kirchner Girl', in black lace 'scanties'. Thus, on display, painted, etched, photographed in poses often too revealing for my liking, she was never out of my sight nor thoughts, either in our home (with its unlisted telephone number) or in the outside world she so adorned. In the course of time the wife and the picture, the real and the unreal, became confused and our private relationship merged with the public image, so that I too became as a man chasing a dream; a man watching the shadow of wind on water. She was everything most dangerous in a woman; intelligent, beautiful, wildly unpredictable and *married to me*. We had lived in splendour and loved fiercely, armed with daggers of unkind words; and each time the kisses took longer to heal the wounds. Like actors we played our parts against the moving European scene until the words we spoke meant no more than the movement of our lips. The coward in me shrank from analysing my feelings towards her, but it was the moments of unhappiness so bitterly experienced that faded before the more vivid hours of laughter and kisses. I had incessantly to guard myself against these regrets, *mi-sec mi-raisin* haunting me like some Mozartian phrase that the heart remembers though the mind forgets. Probably I was more in love with memories, but I was soon to learn that the heart was a tough animal like a dog that could adapt itself to any new owner.

So when, on my return to London, I spoke on the telephone

asking her to send me some clothes to the Guards' Club the words came from lips cold and waxy. She asked me to give her a puppy dog (a sort of substitute for me, I presumed) but instead I sent her roses, glorious but short-lived as our love: the show was over and I was determined not to play the actor who carries on his rôle even when the curtain has long dropped.

Falling in love and out of love is an act of fate; but for me there is always something magical about someone I have been in love with.

At this time I was like a man caught between sleeping and waking, a condition not altogether unpleasant, since every new unhappiness is a new experience, and I was prepared to believe that without sorrow there was no beauty in life. I was not yet 30, but I could say with a poet, whose name I cannot recall, '*J'ai plus de souvenirs que si j'avais mille ans.*' It was not good pretending I wanted it any other way; once more life was guiding me into a luxurious and pleasing vagabondage. I could sleep comfortably in a different bed every night of my life, the choice to be made preferably by myself. My suitcases, faithful companions, would in any event be more practical than the elegant cedar-lined cupboards at the house in Ennismore Street. Regular meals and the knowledge that someone is waiting can have a deadening effect on a man's spirits; he should only very occasionally answer the summons 'Dinner is served' and he should rise to the sound of the gong only reluctantly. Let him eat when he is hungry and drink when he is thirsty; in short he should lead a dog's life, as far as possible, against a moving background. I cannot pretend I was unhappy in my independence; temporarily life was sweet without the pile of household bills on the marble-top table in the hall. Let the postman leave his letters: they were not for me; and let the telephone ring: it was for someone else. Homeless, but not forlorn, with no illusions about a man living by bread alone, I decided to stay at the Guards' Club, an establishment within easy distance of my kindly tailors, Johns and Pegg, my splendid shirtmaker, Eduard and Butler of Cork Street and the Rue de Rivoli, while other long-suffering tradesmen friends were handy in Bond Street and still ready to welcome me with sorrow but no anger.

I was one of a large family (unassailable within my own herd) so I had never become a 'clubman', as known to my generation.

Most men used a club when they wanted company; I used mine when I wished to be alone; where unarmed I could surrender myself and half-close my eyes in the dim-lit corner of a coffee-room redolent of Havana and leather well-worn, the smell of a Muscovite droshky. But clubs were changing since my father's day: already ladies were being admitted as guests to a few clubs, but on sufferance. Some resistance had come, needless to say, from the married members. There was a story that on hearing Queen Mary had been invited into the Pavilion at Lord's after a Test match, a member of the M.C.C. was heard gloomily to mutter, 'This is the thin edge of the wedge.' White's Club has never admitted ladies. I was there with my brother Tristram one evening in the bar when we were joined by Rupert Belville, cosmopolitan, ladies' man, friend of Hemingway and killer of bulls himself. Later, after we'd downed a few drinks Belville said, 'I suppose I should be getting along—I've a taxi waiting.'

Tristram said, 'You've already been here an hour; why don't you pay it off?'

'I would if I could but I can't,' Rupert replied. 'I've Mussolini's daughter in it.'

It is of this club that the story is told that Cyril Connolly, then a newly-joined member, was washing his hands in the appointed place when he found that the nailbrush was firmly screwed to the side of the basin. 'I see you don't trust members very far,' he remarked jocularly to the venerable custodian. 'That brush, sir,' he replied with the dignity possessed only by crowned heads and club servants, 'was the property of General Sir Blasket Torken Hallington, V.C., K.C.M.G., who lost an arm at the Battle of Paardeburg Drift, many years before you were born, sir.' So it is that now, whenever that distinguished *homme de lettres* feels the promptings of nature, he pops over to the Ritz.

I was lunching one day at the R.A.C. (known as 'The Chauffeurs' Arms') as the guest of a man with whom I was only slightly acquainted. He complained so bitterly about the cooking that I suggested he should write to the secretary, to which he replied: 'I certainly would if I was a member.'

Staying at the Guards' Club was still a comfortable experience because the valeting was of the highest standard. During a stay of three nights, a member could have twenty suits or more sponged and pressed and as many shoes and topboots cleaned and polished to perfection by a process known only to the Brigade of Guards, or possibly the cavalry.

I had a second club in St James's, whose members came from every level of society—actors, artists, journalists, sporting men and even financiers. It was also whispered that it was the refuge for a coven of struck-off solicitors and a flock of unfrocked clergy. One thing all shared in common was appreciation of the cooking and of the wine laid down in the club cellars, said to be the envy of Berry Brothers, their neighbours.

There was one member who seemed as permanent as the club furniture. I never refused his invitation to sit with him because although I couldn't like him, he had a vast knowledge (of the bitter-sweet variety), so I would sit silent and listen even though I realized that he was a man without pity. I couldn't help admiring him for the inattention he paid to any conversation on my part. I might have been a better pupil but I had begun to realize that he was a man with the wrong kind of laughter. If strings for a musical instrument had been made out of his guts and mine, those of a wolf and a dog, the sound produced could have never been anything but a discord. Some secret bitterness was eating into him, so that he was neither a man's man, nor a woman's either. In his talk one was always conscious of underlying anger, and when he wished to assume a light-hearted manner it always came out as sarcastic and ill-humoured.

'Never be ashamed to ask,' he advised me one day; but he couldn't help adding, 'The answer you'll get won't be any more stupid than your question.' When anyone joined us he would lean towards me confidentially, cup his hand and hiss in a loud Shakespearian aside, 'Who the hell's this old geezer?'—or—'What the devil's the man talking about?'

He was completely insensitive to other people's feelings, yet I found his company engaging and I sought him out as eagerly as others avoided him. He was not unlike pure alcohol, which is without taste or smell but whose absence in a drink would be sadly missed.

He had a ready wit but for personal reasons I often found it misguided. He had also an unpleasant way of being where he was not supposed to be, and therefore seeing what he was not expected to see. One day he said, 'I'm glad you enjoy street processions and public displays.'

'On the contrary,' I replied, 'I don't like them.'

'Oh!' he said. 'You surprise me, because only last week I was watching the Lord Mayor's Show and I saw you lifting up a very pretty girl so she could see over the heads of the crowd; and it seemed to me that you were doing it with great enthusiasm.' He was like a man living in a wintry Swiss valley whom the sun reached only for a few hours per annum, a man more at home at funerals than at weddings.

He usually sat in a chair from where he could watch the smoke-room entrance; and he reminded me of a well-bred, well-groomed Dalmatian, for looking at him closely one day I saw that he was a study in black and white. From his white head to his bright black shoes, from his immaculate white shirt, his satin sable tie and white pearl tie pin, black ebony holder and white cigarette; in every detail of fashion he was the perfect London clubman of the Year of Grace 1926. His face was deeply scarred, presumably with battle honours; in those days after the Great War, although there were few of us whose flesh had not been outraged by flame, steel or gunshot, it 'wasn't done' to speak of it.

His misanthropic philosophy of life was an excellent antidote to my candidean belief that everything might possibly be for the best. I had heard him turn on people who annoyed him: when he did his language had a scorching quality not unlike the caress of a bunsen burner. Once he said, looking at me rather pointedly, 'Ordinary people [I just managed to slip in 'Speak for yourself' as he continued] should always regard every stranger as a potential enemy whose capacity for harming you has not been measured.' In an unexpectedly kindly moment, he remarked, 'The history of man is one of errors and misunderstandings, but don't forget, young man, I'll always be ready to give *you* advice however deplorable, or squalid your problem may be.' Another time he advised me to avoid attachments to very attractive girls because it made the inevitable moment of parting more painful. 'Self-inflicted pain should be avoided at all costs.' He was not my idea of a lovable man, but it is possible he would have liked to have been. I had already learned that you cannot understand a man until you know the sort of man he'd like to be. In an unrevealing way he invariably spoke well of himself, which was understandable as this was the subject in which he was most interested. I liked him best when he was at his sourest and the invariable undercurrent of anger in his conversation was under control.

He usually sat with his back to the window so that his body threw a dark shadow over the table and even the glasses lost their glitter.

'Try to be honest with a girl, young man, and it is just possible she may be honest with you,' he said one day when he was in good form. 'Before entering into any semi-permanent relationship (there is, of course, no permanent one) the girl must be made to realize that you must have your own way on every occasion and on every occasion it is you who comes first.'

It was difficult to imagine myself mustering the courage to say that to any girl—it was far more likely that the girl would say it to me—but I realized that this sort of ruthless attitude might appeal to his type of woman; he claimed to be a busy man (as if there was something magical about it) though I never saw any evidence of it. Then one day, unexpectedly, because he was as secret as a shuttered house about his own life, I realized he was about to tell me something that might reveal the reason for his bitterness.

'I was a student at Heidelberg when I first met my wife,' he began. 'I used to believe in love at first sight . . . when I first saw her she was standing on the terrace under the castle looking down at the Neckar flowing past the old town; and when I spoke to her my German was sufficiently halting to encourage her to help me out, which she did with enormous charm. She tried to suppress her laughter, but it showed all too plainly in her eyes. After that we used to meet often and each time I left ever more deeply in love.

'Naturally I had a rival, a student princeling out of the *Almanach de Gotha* with quarterings on his coat-of-arms like a checker board. He must have looked up my humble entry in *Debrett* and decided it was not beneath his dignity to challenge me to a duel—this he immediately did on some most trivial pretext.

'He insisted that I'd laughed at him or the Kaiser, or both . . . I only knew I had to accept the challenge, you understand, I'd no alternative as an Englishman and all that; I'd never held a sabre in my life. I persuaded friends to act as my seconds and we set off for the gymnasium where the duel was to be fought.

I'll admit I didn't like it—I didn't like it at all. He was there with his seconds—and a doctor—waiting for me. We put on padded jerkins and head masks which protected the eyes and nose, the cheeks remained exposed; but it was some comfort to know there was a limit to how much he could carve me up. It was just before he put on his visor that I first saw his eyes; I mean, saw his eyes clearly. They were ice-blue and the only expression in them was one of cold hatred: then I knew for certain he was out to kill me if he could get away with it.' He touched the scars on his cheeks with a swift gesture. 'I was on the defensive all the time, fending his blade or hopelessly trying to beat it away from my face but, as you see, he sliced me at will.

'Moreover, he cut me the way he wanted to cut me but he couldn't reach my eyes. Eventually the doctor stopped the fight. He won the duel but I won the girl.' For a moment he paused thoughtfully, 'Or did I? We were married a few months later and we were supremely happy and in due course a man-child came along and that was the end of the marriage.'

'What happened?' I asked.

For a moment he looked at me angrily, as if he regretted having told me anything. 'Too many words can spoil a story,' he said sourly; 'but if you must know . . .' he paused with an ill-humoured upward glance, then very slowly he said, 'I didn't like the child's ice-blue eyes, or the expression of cold hatred in them.' Then he made that dismissive gesture I'd noticed so often when he wished to break off a conversation.

There was a delightful old man with whom I used to discuss books and the topics of the day, but it was a long time before I got any closer to him. I learned that he was chairman of the Food and Wine Committee, so one Easter Sunday I gave him a pair of Georgian silver coasters from Vietche's in St James's and from then on he never ceased to instruct me in the art of gastronomy. He confessed he was not a cook himself. 'It's sufficient,' he said, 'to know how a dish should taste—no chef worth his salt will expect someone else to do the cooking—you don't have to work on the plantation to know whether the coffee tastes good.'

One day when I returned to London, having been abroad for some months, he wasn't at the club, so I enquired of the hall porter. 'I'm sorry to say he's dead, sir.' That was all he would tell but from others I learned that in the City, where he had been 'something of a swell', his affairs had gone wrong, and he had been having a thin time. The club waived his subscription and he continued as chairman of the Food and Wine Committee. He had arrived at the club daily as usual but he no longer dined or lunched there, nor did he accept invitations to do so. Most of the day he spent alone in the reading-room where they found him on the rare occasions when he was wanted on the telephone.

A member of his committee told me: 'He was a very sick man, and got so thin he became all skin and bone. He still took our meetings, knew his food all right, a real gourmet. But he gave up eating here; suppose he found a better place.'

They found him one night when the club was closing; he was seated in his usual chair in the reading-room, but he was dead. When his pockets were searched for his address, all they found was a shilling and a kipper rolled in a newspaper.

Before leaving to join my brother-in-law in the South of France I dined with Bob Rankin. Though he was many years my senior we had both served in the Irish Guards; he was intelligently unconventional and an excellent companion in any company. That night I found him in a very excitable state. 'I've nowhere to play snooker,' he shouted. He explained that he had just presented a full-size billiards table to his club, Arthur's. Unfortunately, the next day for some trivial reason, he had resigned. Worse still, the committee had now told him that if he left the club he would have to leave the billiards table as well. That evening he was so genuinely sad and lonely that I telephoned Louis, in Cannes, who was delighted with the suggestion that I should bring him along.

The next day we left the fogs of London and rode the Blue Train to the sunshine and the 'mimosa-scented coast'. For me it was a big step from 'life on the ocean wave' as a deckhand to life on the Côte d'Azur as a non-paying guest. Weakly I had accepted Louis's invitation without hesitation and prepared to take up my playboy life where I had left it off.

Louis's villa was staffed by Eugène, an old French butler, who also valeted us, Maria, the cook, and her friend Jeanne, *femme de chambre*. There were also two *bonnes-à-tout-faire*, two greyhounds and a superbly idle gardener who picked flowers for the villa in the morning and spent the rest of the day rolling black Algerian tobacco into cigarettes and blowing kisses to the maids.

Maria was a *cordon bleu*: her sauces were superb, which didn't escape the attention of Bob Rankin, who was a gourmet of the first order. Unfortunately Eugène, the butler, detested Maria, the cook. They were like oil and water, rum and claret, or more simply cat and dog.

When Eugène at dinner displayed a dish to Nancy before handing it round the table he would announce, '*Sole Véronique*', then to his mistress but loud enough, unfortunately, for all to hear, he would hiss, '*Dégoutant . . . absolument détestable, ne le mangez pas, chère Madame, je vous en prie.*'

A few days after our arrival Bob's life fell into so unusual a routine that we couldn't help noticing it, because he began dressing every evening in complete evening clothes, white tie and tail coat. He had also unpacked a top hat which he wore throughout dinner. At eleven o'clock punctually a taxi arrived; and he was driven off to some mysterious destination from which he was, as it were, 'returned' by his driver in the early hours of the morning. Friends dining with us were always rather surprised at his festive appearance and the way he quizzed his old timepiece every few minutes like a man with a train to catch. They were, naturally, too polite to show it.

We assumed he was enjoying a love affair which, like Dama da Noche and jasmine with their exquisite perfume, only came into full bloom at night; or like those other flowers that droop their heads all day and only open their petals when darkness falls. We noticed he had taken to spending the whole day in his room, coming down to the salon only when Eugène brought in the evening cocktail tray, an entrance which Bob had timed to the second. The mystery might have continued indefinitely had not Louis's friend, the Baron de Saint-Marc, president of the *Cercle Nautique*, come to luncheon one day. Bob as usual ate alone in his room and, remarking on his absence, Saint-Marc told us the reason of his nightly disappearances.

It appeared that one night Bob had visited a small cabaret in Cannes where, after having drunk an unspecified amount of champagne, he elected to sing 'The Man Who Broke the Bank at Monte Carlo'. His song and subsequent dance had a success so great that he volunteered to repeat the performance the following night: the patron was only too delighted, especially as Bob had been as generous in uncorking bottles for others as he had been for himself. As a result this sordid little night club, well patronized by Bob's numerous Etonian friends and with the strongest support from visiting Parisians, had become the smartest *boîte* in Cannes.

Bob was delighted when he heard his fame had spread: and now his secret was out he had no hesitation in inviting us to see his act. He certainly put on a wonderful performance. He had, in fact, done a remarkable thing, for despite his unmusical voice and his uncertain steps, with his tail coat, white tie, top hat, stick and gloves, he had persuaded the hard-boiled Riviera audience that it was no artiste they were watching but the actual man in person who had broken the bank at Monte Carlo for two million francs and more.

Unfortunately, there was a gallery at one end of the club, about twenty feet from the floor, from which he was often persuaded to jump. Twice we saw him do it, fortunately without injuring himself. It was actually a remarkable feat for a man of nearly fifty, and though I have always been aware of the cushioning effect champagne can produce, I still deplored this dangerous *salto mortale* which had now become part of his turn; and I could rarely sleep until I had heard his driver decant him at the front door.

Eventually I had to ask Nancy to plead with him to cut out what, in my nightmare imaginings, actually became the death-leap. When Bob realized the anxiety he was causing, he immediately promised to abandon the acrobatics, for he was one of the kindest and most considerate of men.

Fortunately he himself began to realize that he was drinking too much both before and after his turn. We had already noticed that he had also fallen into the habit of dropping off to sleep during dinner; and on several occasions he had been quite angry when Eugène had discreetly nudged him awake with the dish he was serving. But it was without any further prompting that he decided to hand in his notice. His *patron* on bended knees begged and even attempted to bribe him to remain, but Bob resisted all offers, giving as the reason that he had no wish to blackleg and keep a professional artiste out of a job.

The cabaret survived Bob's departure only a short time, for

his audience had come to love him just as everyone did; but I never quite knew how his disappointed *patron* felt about him.

In Cannes I was soon recognized as the odd man, so beloved of society hostesses, so I was welcome in many villas and invited to parties from which many brilliant and eligible young men were often excluded. There was motley hanging in my cupboards and a variety of masks, for like most people I hid behind my *persona*.

But I had many genuine friends, two of the most important of which were Fred and Eric, who served the drinks at the Casino; and acted as bankers when our luck was out at the tables. However, the *vin ordinaire* and black Algerian tobacco tasted as good to me in the proletarian hovels of Le Suquet as the champagne and coronas in the hillside villas on the Californie.

Duncan Orr-Lewis, the playboy millionaire baronet and Grenadier, was a constant companion. At this period his love affairs (both casual and serious and conducted largely in his 200-ton yawl *Volonté*) were so complicated that it took someone of my romantic-realistic temperament to help him sort them out. To maidens in distress Duncan was the knight errant *par excellence*, even when their distress was more dubious than dire. One evening I was talking to quite the loveliest girl at a party when suddenly she was called away. As she came back I saw the colour had gone from her cheeks and even her eyes.

She had just received a *pneu* (the equivalent of an English telegram, only slower) telling her that her lover, a wealthy industrialist, had died in the apartment they shared together in Paris. Much as she loved the deceased she had also a soft spot for her jewels and furs left in the apartment. Under the *Code Napoléon* the wife or next of kin was entitled to everything she could lay her hands on. There was no time to be lost, she had to get there first.

With unusual presence of mind I enlisted the services of Duncan, a really fast driver with, invariably, the fastest car of any parked outside a party. He drove the stricken damsel to Paris in under eight hours, arriving at the apartment twenty minutes before the wife, who had travelled by *rapide* from Aix-les-Bains, where she had been spending the weekend with her lover. Duncan was not a man to seek favours, but on this occasion I felt he deserved any that came his way.

One of our greatest friends was Florence de Pena, a titian-haired American woman of irresistible personality and a tireless hostess. She was a beautiful woman, married to a monstrously wealthy Argentinian, and at that time was as a sort of sideline mistress of the King of Spain. She probably liked me because I moved in no definite circles and went only where it amused me to go.

One night she invited me to dine with her at the Casino, asking me to be on time, *hora inglesa*. When I arrived she immediately told me to order sixty double dry martinis. As she had previously told me that we were dining *à deux* I suggested that the order was flattering to my reputation as a bibber but on the large side; she explained that at the last hour she had invited twenty-eight other guests.

To celebrate my birthday or hers, I forget whose, she gave me a pair of cufflinks of diamonds, emeralds and onyx, a combination of precious and semi-precious stones that Van Cleef, the Place Vendôme jewellers, had made famous. She was a kindly if conspicuous spender. Money had not only to be spent; but had to be seen to be spent.

Count Zabrowski and Babe Barnato (sponsors of the Chitty Chitty Bang Bang and the Bentley), both compulsive pleasure seekers, used to be around in those days and there were some uncomfortably exciting drives between Nice and Monte Carlo in the early morning hours: the *moyen Corniche* had become a sort of race track for the *jeunesse dorée*. Zabrowski's father had killed himself on this glorious ledge and the son eventually re-enacted the fatal event at, I believe, exactly the same bend, though not in his Chitty Chitty Bang Bang. He was so fond of new cars it used to be said of him that he bought a new one as soon as the ashtray on the old one was full. Babe was the first of the playboys to go hatless: he estimated it saved him a thousand a year in cloakroom tips.

Shortly after my arrival I encountered a Greek friend who lived in Paris and was famous for doling out very small gratuities. He was as mean with servants as Louis Drexel was generous. It is, of course, a well-known fact that to afford to be mean a man must be very, very wealthy, and my friend had not really even this excuse.

One evening he was giving a dinner party for twelve in his

suite at the Carlton. As I had arrived early he invited me to inspect the table, a very honourable request which also gave me an opportunity to rearrange the place cards so I would be seated next to the most attractive woman.

The table decorations, carnations and gardenias, which I had previously suggested, were perfect. Father had taught me the order of flowers: lilacs in the hall, roses in the drawing-room and carnations in the dining-room.

Then I noticed that, because of his meanness, the kitchen staff had taken a most Machiavellian revenge. (The shape of bread-rolls, in all countries, is based in varying degrees on the male or female principle. This is traditional, and derives from the pastry-cooks of ancient Rome.) The normal feminine rolls had been placed on the plates engraved with the men's names; and to the ladies rolls had been distributed of such grossly phallic proportions as to be neither more (and certainly not less) than the *penis erectus*. Amused, but to avoid embarrassment, I ordered toast Melba to be substituted. As dinner progressed, I saw my host in the best of form quite unaware of what had happened, while I, instead of enjoying the discourse and the music of popping champagne corks, ate sparingly, apprehensive, wondering what other and more devilish revenge the kitchen staff might have devised.

At this time the Riviera was attracting the many American writers and painters whose credit had run out at the Select, the Flore, the Coupole and the Deux Magots in Paris. They had crossed the Atlantic in search of European culture. The love-hate relationship between Hemingway and Scott Fitzgerald had reached the point where it placed a considerable strain on friendship to be in the same town, let alone the same bar, with them. Scott had helped Hemingway to find a publisher but suffered the usual fate of benefactors: he was dropped. It seemed as if Hemingway never forgave Scott for helping him nor himself for his own ingratitude; but it was Scott who carried the more obvious chip on his shoulder. Someone once said to Liam O'Flaherty: 'I met so-and-so who was blackguarding you most outrageously.' 'That's strange,' replied Liam, 'I never remember doing the fellow a good turn.'

Under the veneer of the cosmopolitan man of the world there peered the wondering eyes of a little show-off boy from the

Middle West; I was always under the impression that while Hemingway had memorized the wine list backwards, Scott still couldn't read the menu.

At first I was regarded by this American expatriate *côterie* as an amiable Englishman and a shadowy figure about whom they knew little and cared less; though their interest was undoubtedly stimulated when they realized that I could be relied upon to ante-up at each recurring financial crisis.

Like myself they were in search of the raw material of life about which to write. Then one night I realized they had opened their ragged ranks and I was among friends; maybe they had seen reflected in my eyes a glimmer of strange things I had seen; and recognized through the laughter and the tears that I was *à côté*, if not actually one of them.

None of this little group included what could be described as the natural eccentric. The Scott Fitzgeralds, who were staying with their long-suffering friends the Murphys, were wild; and Scott himself was exhibitionist rather than eccentric. Brash and truculent on meeting someone for the first time, he was never satisfied until he'd qualified the introduction by: 'Yes, I'm Scott Fitzgerald, the world-famous alcoholic.' With his odious manners and great talent as a writer, he was a money snob ready at the drop of a hat to raise his own hat to the rich. Yet he was a kinder man than Hemingway and could write, 'In the dark night of the soul it is always three o'clock in the morning.'

I knew of only one man there who attempted the heights of true eccentricity, an Englishman as one would expect. He was the retired colonel of a crack cavalry regiment (crack because he wouldn't have accepted second-best), and possessed some of the necessary attributes; though his conventional Victorian upbringing weighed heavily against him. Once a month he strove to break the mould that imprisoned him; but, alas, he always failed and was finally brought to the level of the common man.

He loved France in spite of 'the frogs and all those sauces they covered the food in, the hand-kissing', and what he described in general all-round terms as 'all the mounseer nonsense'.

He often gave dinner parties (to which I was invited) in his suite at the Gray and Albion Hotel. These parties (black tie and dinner jacket *obligatoire*) would have been the essence of Victorian conventionality and decorum, were it not for the fact that the

Dora Lady Grayson

Father as usual riding high 'where the princes ride at noon'

Ravenspoint

Rooftop dining now and then
Is relished by the wisest men
But most, I hope, when I am host

lady guests were naked, except for their shoes, jewellery and the handbags from which they refused to be parted. The Colonel, in the best military tradition, recruited them from the most reliable and discreet establishments in Nice.

'I'd have had Rubens here if he'd lived in this century,' he whispered to me on one occasion as he assessed the assembled female curves, adding: 'In the circumstances I only intend saying a short grace.'

At dinner the food, wine and cigars were excellent but the conversation was rather forced, and lacked that freedom of expression usual at dinner parties on a higher social scale; for risqué stories were, on the Colonel's orders, taboo. Sometimes he would call me aside and say: 'What an appalling crowd of people, I can't think where they come from.' This sort of remark, made probably to everyone in turn, was ridiculous because no one was admitted without showing an engraved card, *Requesting the pleasure of the company of* . . . and terminating in the crisp reminder, *Carriages 11.30 p.m.*

At 11.15 the ladies would be helped into their fur coats and the party would break up. The Colonel never understood why his parties failed to take off—and none liked to tell him that the propriety he insisted upon was completely out of date, and his idea of bohemia far too strict. After one of these dinners he asked me why his parties always hung fire. I didn't wish to offend him, but it was noticeable that even Harry Melville (as brilliant a conversationalist and homosexual as Wilde himself), with all the opportunities for talk embosomed, you might say, within this captive audience, seemed to have left his wits at his villa. I suggested that some sort of mild distraction might help.

'You mean a conjurer or someone doing card tricks?' he asked.

'No, but you might perhaps engage an orchestra.'

'What, turn it into a musical soirée—Chopin and that lot?'

'No, I meant dance music, Viennese waltzes and. . . .'

'Oh, no,' he interrupted, 'that would never do, not my idea of *comme il faut* at all.'

There must be some instinctive aversion from public nudity, inherited probably from Adam and Eve who, if one can believe the accounts, were quickly on with the fig leaf when the snake appeared. I have noticed at nudist camps on the Ile du Levant and at the lakeside establishments at Wannsee outside Berlin that except for isolated family groups there was an uncanny absence of sustained conversation; and even the hard-breathing vegetarian professional nudists devoted their energies exaggeratedly to ball games. I therefore suggested that the *nu intégral* was a trifle formidable and it might be a good idea to introduce the *câche sexe*. Very angrily he replied, 'I'll have no money transactions at my parties.'

I used to play squash or golf occasionally at Mandalieu but with my dislike of games played with a ball (of any size) I went more for the company than the play; but there were no ball games at the Colonel's parties, as he disapproved of anything that might be described as romping.

With un-English stubbornness, he refused to compromise, and though he wished to be an eccentric he was never regarded as more than unconventional.

Gradually the acceptances dwindled and through lack of attendance he was forced to discontinue his parties. It was a sad blow to his esteem as he was genuinely hospitable and never so happy as when entertaining.

One evening, at a very different type of party, I met Margaret Coats, daughter of the cotton millionaire. She was more than beautiful and exercised on me such overwhelming and immediate charm that when I was first introduced I stood speechless. I was never to meet her again; but if by some chance she reads these lines she will learn that a young man, of whose existence she seemed unaware, spent many hours in a grove of mimosa on the Californie opposite the drive gates of her home in the hope of catching even a glimpse of her. Years later I heard that this beautiful lady had married Edgie Knollys, who was at Harrow with me.

No young man should be without a shrine at which to grieve; and it was important for me to experience the complete exhilaration of unhappiness and to learn to appreciate the exquisite pains of martyrdom.

I was lucky to find my Irish Guards comrade, Valentine Williams, living in Cannes. He himself was a first-class detective and thriller writer and had created an infamous character in a series of thrillers called *The Man with the Club Foot*. This universally loathed chief of German Intelligence makes any of

Fleming's villains look mildly childish, and Valentine's characters really knew the shadow world of the secret agent; and the high world, when they lived it up. There was none of the guide-book culture and fake sophistication displayed by James Bond and his co-evils.

Encouraged by Valentine, I now became seriously engaged upon my book and felt a real thrill as the plot unravelled itself and the characters came to life. I used the background of Cannes and Monte Carlo and the lonely heights above the Gorge du Loup and Gourdon where anything might happen and usually did. To my astonishment the work progressed.

Often we would visit Louis Drexel's father on his magnificent yacht *Sayonara*. Tony had converted her from steam to oil and installed bathrooms beside every cabin. The yacht was completely furnished with Louis XV pieces standing on Aubusson carpets. With exquisite furnishings and hangings he was always able to obtain the finest charters; because the women of the jet set looked for luxury and comfort and Tony knew it was the wife or mistress who finally decided.

One day we were a party of twenty people on board for luncheon. The meal was not served before two o'clock, so an elegant sufficiency of champagne cocktails had been drunk. After the caviare an entrée was served. I noticed a second steward was following with a silver dish of brussels sprouts. Suddenly Tony leapt to his feet. Red in the face, he ordered the man to throw the contents of the dish out of the port-window. It would have been asking too much even of these well-conditioned people to have shown no reaction to their host's unexpected outburst at the appearance of a dish of sprouts, so what might be described as a well-bred silence, lasting no more than seconds, fell on the company.

Then his daughter, Margaretta (married to Lord Winchelsea) asked very sweetly, 'But how do you know some of us don't like brussels sprouts, Pa?'

Tony had seated himself and in a voice now perceptibly controlled announced: 'No one eats brussels sprouts in any establishment of mine, afloat or ashore,' and pointing to the bearded Grand Duke Michael, uncle of Tsar Nicholas and grandfather of the late Lord Milford Haven, 'not even you, Michael, sir.' What was all this about? Tony, good-looking, healthily bawdy, with a hundred thousand a year (and always grumbling because he couldn't touch the capital), pleasure-loving, with Scholte suits, Maxwell shoes, Fabergé cigarette case, rivalling even those of the Grand Duke—how did it come about that this American extrovert should insist on the destruction of a few brussels sprouts?

I saw the look of anxious concern on the face of Van Vouris, his friend and secretary, when Tony's angry eyes turned on him; and then he smiled. Suddenly everything was back to normal, the Waterford glass twinkled and the silver shone again; conversation flowed, light laughter followed, the play had been resumed and all were back in their parts. But with me the nagging question was still there. Were the sprouts too plebeian for the guests or were they too good for them? Had, perhaps, this homely vegetable played a part in the tragic history of the Romanovs? Now a beautiful calm had fallen on the saloon, not unlike the quiet music that follows the storm in that monstrous overture to *Poet and Peasant*.

We drank our coffee seated under an awning on the afterdeck where cigars and liqueurs were served. I was near the Grand Duke when I noticed Sir Hugo de Bathe approaching, limping heavily on his stick. Suddenly the Grand Duke, angrily drawing in his feet, commanded: 'Be careful with that stick, Sugy!' Whereupon Sir Hugo raised his stick very slowly, and said: 'Have no fear, your Imperial Highness, I wouldn't even touch you with the end of it.' Why this hatred? Was the Grand Duke annoyed because Sugy had wooed and won the Jersey Lily and ex-mistress of Edward VII, Lily Langtry, or was this display of rudeness a form of royal behaviour, or was it a side-effect from the incident of the brussels sprouts?

Some weeks later Tony volunteered a fairly reasonable explanation of this episode, considering that, like most millionaires, he followed only his own likes and dislikes. 'As a boy I was sent to a school in Brussels,' he explained, 'and I've hated Brussels ever since. Now I find it impossible to be friendly with anyone who likes anything even vaguely connected with the damned place.'

It was beginning to seem to me that the characters in my book, even though imaginary, behaved more like real people than some of the real people I moved among.

One afternoon I was on the spiral descent from Pera Cava, the Alpes Maritimes winter-sports village, with Scott and Zelda Fitzgerald. We stopped at the last patch of white and, like children, piled all the snow we could carry on to the car so we could drive under the palms into the sunshine of Cannes with the roof all white and glittering. On arrival we made for the nearest civilized bar and when some hours later we were emptied on to the Croisette, Zelda cried piteously and rather noisily when she saw that her precious snow had melted. A crowd quickly gathered, believing no doubt that we were ill-treating her; and we had to drive quickly off. And a few minutes later our voices were in unison, singing and echoing along the Rue d'Antibes. We dined that night in a country restaurant late, as all people should in vine countries where the workers return home late from the vineyards; and that night these two exhibitionists were silenced, it seemed, by the perfume of the eucalyptus and the beauty of the night. Or was it because we were all too drunk to laugh and talk any longer? *Où sont les neiges d'antan*? Only of this I was certain: the only sane people I seemed to know between Cannes and Monte Carlo were my hosts Nancy and Louis, the gardener blowing his kisses to the maids, and those coming to life in my book.

I could usually bath and dress and take my *café complet* in about an hour and a half; but Louis took at least four hours to rise and dress. He was very methodical, took enormous care with his appearance and resisted any attempts to hurry him. He was as unpunctual as a gambler and could only be relied upon to be late for meals. He rarely drank anything until six o'clock in the evening: then he started on champagne which he continued drinking until three o'clock in the morning, or later if he could persuade me or my like to join him.

Most mornings his three children would be driven to the Croisette where they played with their friends and where all the nannies (mostly English) would congregate.

I would work on my book at the end of the garden under the resin-scented pines. Here beyond the white balustrade I could see Les Lerins lying like low green clouds over the blue waters. It was really too lovely a place to work in. Robert Hichens, author of the best-selling *Garden of Allah*, had a pavilion built in the garden of his villa at Territet with a beautiful view over Lake

Geneva. So beautiful indeed, he told me, that eventually he could only work with the curtains drawn.

One morning, while I was at work, Eugène summoned me urgently to the villa where I found a sergeant of police. He wanted to see Mr Drexel. There is nothing less agreeable than an uninvited guest at 10.30 a.m., especially when he is in uniform. Fortunately, Eugène, who always knew the form, arrived with a tray of drinks and this immediately lifted the interview on to a civilized, if not convivial, plane. It appeared that the maids, Jeanne and Marie, had been visiting the casino in the afternoons playing with *jetons* of large denomination. They had quickly come under the observation of the *Chef de Partie*, who had reported it to the police. It was clear to the police that their gambling was no more than a pretext to convert the *jetons* into hard cash. They had been followed: hence his presence at the villa. Before taking action he wished to know whether Mr Drexel could throw any light on how they came to be in possession of the *jetons*, which he was now carrying in his black satchel.

At once I realized that if it was proved that they had no right to the *jetons* the law would take its course, and hundreds of hours would be wasted in evil-smelling courts to the sound of scratching official pens, culminating in a trial with the probability of long terms of imprisonment for Jeanne and Marie. In short, the alarming fact was at once apparent—we were about to lose Marie, our magnificent cook, our *cordon bleu*, to say nothing of Jeanne, who would accompany her into captivity.

With rare quickness of wit I explained that I would have to consult with Mr Drexel, who had not as yet awakened; so it was arranged that the sergeant should return at four o'clock after luncheon. Moreover, to keep things sweet (like his aperitifs which Eugène had just replenished), I assured him a satisfactory explanation would be forthcoming.

When I told Nancy what had happened she was as alarmed as I had been, realizing immediately that her domestic arrangements were threatened. At all costs the law must be kept out of the kitchen. Eugène, who had naturally heard everything, was shaking his head, mumbling countless *mon dieu*s and rolling his eyes to the ceiling, muttering, '*Ces femmes . . . ces femmes*'.

Nancy at once decided to hold a 'court of inquiry' and it was a chastened Jeanne and Marie who confessed that they had found the *jetons* in the guest room, even in the bed itself. The temptation to take them had been too much. A tearful scene followed during which they both swore on their parents' graves (subsequently we learned they were still alive) they would never again do such a wicked thing as to steal. Nancy, who was always practical, insisted on a signed confession.

When the sergeant returned I was able to assure him that Madame Drexel was satisfied with the explanation given her by the two maids but that Monsieur Drexel, to offset the trouble the police had been put to, would like him to accept the *jetons* for their Widows' and Children's Fund, or to be used otherwise at their discretion.

To this suggestion the *agent* immediately agreed; but he gave me an understanding look as he accepted the package: the law had not been flouted but adjusted to our mutual advantage. Nancy thus washed her hands of the *jetons* which were shaped in fact like small pieces of soap, and thus known as *savonettes*.

Eugène, contrary to expectations, was delighted, probably because it confirmed his low opinion of female domestic servants, cooks in particular. That night at dinner, as he handed the entrée dish, it was with a smile that he announced: '*L'agneau au casino, pommes roulette et carrottes aux jetons*,' and in his usual loud whisper, '*delicieux, Madame, mangez-en, je vous en prie*.'

Those were great times for me, living with those I loved. The road ahead stretched before me, mysterious and adventurous, life was sweet and spiced with the little sadness that must always be there. On most nights I walked home after some party along the Croisette and I was usually sober enough to see the stars glistening like white flowers in the dark meadows of the Mediterranean sky; and I would be looking forward to those nightly dreams wherein the characters in my book had begun to talk and have their being; and I knew that my beloved old friend would always be awaiting my return with yet another bottle of champagne on the ice.

CHAPTER III

Go litel book, go litel myn tragedie.

CHAUCER

I had finished my book. Never, even in my fondest moments, had I held anything so precious in my hands. It had been written *con amore*, a work of love; and it had given me many hours of happiness and anguish. I felt every sensation a woman, I suppose, must feel when she holds her first miraculous child in her arms; weariness, relief, exultation and love. I had brought my characters to life in the blood and ink of my imagination. For me they lived and sometimes they died (or simply walked out on me even when I believed they were important to the story) and sometimes minor characters only casually conceived would take charge. But one and all were moving in the places wherein they loved and lived, hated and died, dominating my dreams at night. Sometimes I had introduced real people into the book; my intelligence chief, thinly disguised behind the initial X, was clearly recognizable by those who knew Captain Mansfield Comyns.

During the First World War, Mansfield Comyns, an ex-naval officer, had been in charge of our counter-espionage. He had been involved in a motor accident with his son: Comyns had been thrown clear with grave injuries and it was generally understood that he used a jack knife to sever his leg so as to reach his son who lay dying a short distance away. His method of running his secret office in Whitehall Chambers must have inspired the expression 'cloak and dagger' because in spite of his shrewdness, particularly in appointing the right agents for the right work, this cork-legged sailor enjoyed the secrecy and mystery of his strictly unofficial job; and it was only after his death that his name really came to light. Sometimes during an interview he would idly jab a sharply pointed knife into this leg, a masochistic action disconcerting to anyone not in the know. He is the only man I have met who collected telescopes. He had a remarkable array of them which he housed in Portsmouth, a farsighted hobby in more ways than one, as I believe at his death they fetched enormous prices.

However, my next problem was to sell the book. As Colonel Putnam, of the famous American publishing house, told Pat Kirwan, my friend of Berlin days, 'Any fool can write a book but it takes genius to sell it.' I decided to take off for London. My manuscript was far too precious to be entrusted to the French and English postal systems.

A few days before departure I was walking on the Croisette with Nannie and the children when we met another nannie with her charge, a little black-eyed Russian girl holding a small dog. While the nannies talked, the little girl lifted the dog, a griffon, into my arms and we all three made friends. I told the little girl and the nannie how much I liked their dog. Then I hurried on because I had arranged to meet another little girl, but one who had not had a nannie for some years.

Next morning when the children came back from the Croisette they had the little griffon with them and to my surprise it was handed to me. The nannie had told her Russian mistress how much I liked the dog and so she had insisted on my having it. Its name was Luska, 'the lovely one', and in truth I already loved her. The following day I gave the nannie a note to give the Russian lady, together with Luska, for obviously I couldn't accept so quixotic a gift. In the afternoon they came back with Luska; and the following morning I again sent her back. Once more her mistress returned her to me. This time I made up my mind I would keep her; and would have done so had not my niece told me that the nannie and her mistress had been crying their eyes out. Back went Luska; only to be returned later with the message that Monsieur, owing to Madame's distress over Luska, had bought her a blue mink : therefore she had decided to buy a dog that would match her new coat.

As before leaving London my wife had asked me for a puppy dog, I determined she should have this one: the only problem was how to get it to her. It would clearly take a lot of planning for I had no intention of putting Luska into quarantine for six months before she could take up residence in England. I had no qualms about smuggling. Indeed, at that time I was at the height of my career as a customs-evader. I was a compulsive smuggler, though I drew the line at drugs and white slavery. I smuggled only what I needed for myself; but smuggling a dog into England would be a new and tricky experience. I took Luska to the leading veterinary surgeon in Cannes for a thorough examination; she was in perfect health but to reassure me he inoculated her for hydrophobia.

This happened before the days when matching wits with the Inland Revenue had become a national pastime. Smuggling, though not as socially acceptable as banking or cheating the tax inspector, was recognized as an impulse inherent and traditional in our brave island race and therefore permissible if not applaudible. Brandy for the parson, baccy for the clerk, etcetera.

The journey to Paris with Luska was simple, and by the time we reached the Gare de Lyon she had learned to depend on me. It was still winter and I was wearing a heavy fur coat, so I slit the musquash lining and inside this she made a snug little nest for herself in which, as I moved about, she was rocked to sleep.

I intended staying the night in Paris, so I went as part of my plan to the Bristol in the Faubourg St Honoré, where I was unknown. I registered (giving an hotel address in Cannes) and to hide my trail yet more made inquiries about the trains to Biarritz. So far no one in the hotel had seen Luska. I was determined to trust no one. At all costs I must guard against coincidences and chance encounters.

I knew that an exchange information service operated between excise men on both sides of the Channel. A dog seen on the boat train at the Gare du Nord would be immediately reported to the Gare Maritime in Calais, with a full description of anyone accompanying it. If the description answered to someone boarding the ship without a dog, the information would be transmitted to Dover, where a search would be made.

In view of this I decided to travel by air, with Luska concealed from the moment I left Paris, indeed from the night before. I booked my ticket by Air France, whose hostess on board, if the worst came to the worst, would be less concerned than an English one.

I next visited Roberts, that *roi de pharmaciens* in the Rue de la Paix. He was well known as a dispenser of hangover cures to Father's generation and certainly to mine, having ministered for at least three decades to those suffering from wounds self-inflicted at the altar of Bacchus. I asked him guardedly what sedative he would recommend for a small child. He immediately produced a bottle of white sugar liquid which was probably just what the doctor would have ordered. Next morning I tried it out on Luska and was reassured when she licked the cork and liked it.

I then told the hall porter to call a taxi to take me to the Gare d'Orléans. With my manuscript in my capacious pocket and Luska in the lining of my coat, and carrying a travelling rug over my arm to hide the bulge, we started off. I immediately re-routed the cab to the Hotel Danou, where I left my baggage, believing this would simplify my flight. We then drove to the Rue Scribe where we boarded the coach to Le Bourget. I found myself seated next to an American girl. A few minutes after we'd pulled out, to my consternation she remarked coolly, 'Oh my! You've got a dog with you, sir.'

Taking the coach instead of a taxi was mistake number two. Already, quite unwittingly, I had made mistake number one (which did not come to light until my arrival in England) but this second mistake was fortunately not too serious, because the next thing she said was: 'I felt it move—it's only fair to tell you that my aunt was caught trying to smuggle a dog into England last month, and she had to pay £500 or go to prison for three months.'

This was hardly the sort of news I wanted to hear at that moment, but at least I knew that the girl wouldn't give me away.

At Le Bourget it was announced that our flight was delayed. Luska was still fast asleep. The American girl said: 'Now don't worry, do what Pa would do, treat yourself to some iced champagne, light up a cigar and watch all the pretty ladies.' I guided her to a corner table in the restaurant.

This girl was all American except for a pleasant hint of Paris in her Schiaparelli coat and skirt, the Hellstern shoes, and a sprinkling of Cartier's diamonds and emeralds to make her glisten. I had noticed whenever she opened her Hermès handbag the air filled with the delicious fragrance of Guerlain's Russian Leather; in fact, she was a sort of live advertisement for the Faubourg St Honoré, Rue Royale and Rue de la Paix. Though she obviously enjoyed being the onlooker or even mild accomplice in my smuggling she refused to share my champagne, preferring to drink a *citron pressé*. 'That cigar smells wonderful,' she said. This was Cuban music to my ears because it confirmed my theory that Havana tobacco is unique and the grandest of all smells because, unlike the rest, it evokes yet other and entirely dissimilar smells: Roger et Gallet soap, rich cooking and mellow brandy; and even the indescribable aroma of old furniture and royal Bokharas, hanging tapestries, and the Russian leather in a Rolls coupé de ville. Of all smells it is the one that most swiftly evokes all that is most seductive in luxurious living and leisure and loving. That is why all women love the smell of a good cigar.

'What do you do?' she asked suddenly.

'Usually the first thing that comes into my head—unfortunately.'

'I don't mean that, I mean how do you earn your living?'

That was an awkward one when I thought of the handsome allowance Father made me, but I answered boldly: 'I'm a seaman, I go down to the sea in ships and do my business in great waters.'

'Sure, in your fur coat with astrakhan collar and a dog hidden in the lining.'

'I'm sorry if I don't look the part,' I told her. This was true because going to sea before the mast was the only thing I had to be proud of, the only thing since the war I'd done off my own bat, as the cricketers say, though I hadn't been too successful at it. The interesting thing was not how well I'd done it but, as Samuel Johnson said of the lady preacher, that it had been done at all.

'Is that all you've done?' she said.

'Well, I've just finished writing a book.'

Naturally it wasn't the first time I'd noticed how attractive she was—at an early age American girls learn to interest and attract men; and with her blue eyes assuming an expert expression of seriousness and her lips slightly parted she was the epitome in colour and form of the top American cover-girl.

'Written a book! That's thrilling.'

'That's exactly what I hope it is,' I confessed, somewhat nervously, but she continued eagerly: 'With lots of murders in it?'

'I've got a nice contemporary one you'd like and an old-fashioned one to comfort an older generation.'

'You'll promise me a signed copy when it comes out?'

'I will, if I ever find a publisher.'

When she asked me my name she repeated it thoughtfully and said: 'It doesn't ring any bells with me.' I'd seen her own name on her black kid baggage, Carol Carol-Carol. But with a face like hers what's in a few names. We walked together into the customs shed at Croydon and still Luska never moved. Having no luggage I walked directly through with my heart's beat quickening, hiding the bulge in my coat made by Luska with the rug draped over my arm. I was not stopped. I walked down passages where airport police stood at every intersection. At last I came to the exit and waited for the coach. Some minutes later my American friend came through. She made straight for me and whispered breathlessly, 'Don't wait for the coach, flag down a cab.' But her words were almost drowned by the intercom with its spluttering unfriendly voice croaking, 'Mr Grayson is wanted in the customs shed.'

My immediate reaction was that someone had informed on me. I walked back with sinking heart, knowing I was going to be parted from Luska, to say nothing of the £500 fine.

'You're Mr Grayson, you've just travelled on the plane from Paris?'

'Yes.'

'Why didn't you clear customs?'

'I'd no baggage so I just walked through.'

'You just walked through, as simple as that? Well, in future you just report to customs. We've got you down as travelling on the plane and when you don't check here you're adrift. Have you anything to declare?'

'Not a thing,' I answered truthfully; after all, Luska wasn't a thing and my manuscript, though precious beyond rubies and pearls to me, was worthless to these inquisitors. For sixty seconds we looked each other in the eyes.

'Okay,' he said cheerfully, not even reluctantly.

Carol was still waiting for the bus. Actually my long drawn-out agony could have only lasted five minutes. She gave me a shining white smile and a bright blue wink.

This time I called a taxi from the nearby hotel and went to meet it.

In London I took Luska for a walk in Kensington Gardens to revive her after the journey; then from a hat shop in Sloane Street I bought an oval cardboard box into which I popped her, tied it up in ribbon with a large bow, pink for a girl. On a label I wrote, 'Luska, fragile, handle with loving care, definitely this side up.'

I sent a message to my wife to ask her to collect a very important box from the Hyde Park Hotel, just arrived from Paris. What woman could resist that? Later I heard from the lady in the cloakroom how delighted Ruby had been; and Luska, too, I suspect. I had only been a makeshift mother: now she had a real one.

The next day I wrote again to my wife warning her to be discreet about Luska's origin as I'd already had a monstrous note from my brother Denys, suggesting I might be introducing hydrophobia into the country; to which I replied curtly that Luska had been examined in Cannes and passed as fit. I had been dead lucky, and so had Luska of the beautiful name.

Some years later when Prince George, later Duke of Kent, wanted a similar Russian name for his beautiful alsatian bitch, I suggested Duschka. I'd learned to say this, which means 'darling', to my little guide in Russia; and as he loved her he called her that.

I had arranged to dine with Carol at Claridge's that night, so I bought her a flutter of little orchids which she could either wear or pin on to her evening handbag. I was looking forward to meeting her again—together we had already experienced doubt, fear and elation, and we had shared a secret; for a brief space of time we had, as it were, walked together. Had she wished she could have betrayed me to my enemies. Let someone do you a favour and quite possibly you've made a friend. I prayed it might be so with her.

I was quite incapable of feigning indifference to anyone I admired. In the past I had always betrayed my obvious enchantment with a girl but with this spoiled poor little rich girl I meant to play the part of the cool, cold Englishman. The orchids, I persuaded myself, were no more than a conventional gesture and even if I intended ordering a specially good dinner I'd have done that if she'd come from the back row of the chorus.

It was in this (unnaturally for me) calculating mood that I went to meet her. I was in the lounge when she came in, beautiful and glittering and trailing clouds of glory and Chanel.

'What are you doing here?' she asked, just as though we'd met by chance.

'I'm engaged, honourably and as arranged, in the task of ordering dinner for two. Is there anything wrong with that?" I replied.

'In a way, because we're dining in the suite,' she said, and that was exactly where we did dine, not quite tête-à-tête, but with her father, two uncles, a cousin from Devonshire and her old nanny who'd come up from Brighton.

None of them had seen her for a long time, she had a thousand questions to answer and it was obvious that they all loved her, so that even I (annoyed with her as I was) began to feel myself being drawn into this orbit of adoration.

Her father, obviously a most amiable man, steered me to the cocktails and said, 'So you're the man with the dog.' They all seemed to have heard my story because each one of her friends and relatives greeted me with, 'So you're the man with the dog.' Dinner, at which I was separated from Carol by three aunts and two uncles, was hardly over before the door opened and two more friends from Baltimore and yet another cousin from New York arrived. It was time, I decided, that 'the man with the dog' should go. I slipped into the bedroom, took the wilting orchids from my pocket where they had been all evening and placed them on her dressing-table; then let myself out.

Some years later I was taken by friends to a very grand party given by the Marchesa L——— della R——— at her palace in Rome, and saw that my wonderfully gowned and bediamonded hostess, statuesque at the head of a marble staircase, was my accomplice of the airport. As my friends sought to introduce me she put forth both her hands and cried, 'But it's the man with the dog.' Carol Carol-Carol had married above me.

In the meantime in London I still had the problem of my own marriage. As I have said, I had married one of the world's most beautiful women. A Marxist philosopher has said that a problem correctly formulated is a problem already half-solved. My marriage was a problem I could not even envisage, and so I fled from it.

I handed in my manuscript to Eveleigh Nash, who assured me of a prompt reading and decision; and took refuge the while with the poet, Henry Savage, in his tumbledown cottage on Winchelsea beach. Henry had been born in a pub, had fought as a trooper in the South African War (he had considered this less risky than staying to face an irate husband in England), and in those carefree days before World War I had been a friend of Marie Lloyd and Alec Hurley from the music halls, Bernard Dillon and Solly Joel on the turf and Lord Alfred Douglas, W. B. Yeats and Frank Harris, the author of *My Life and Loves*, in the world of letters. Henry was a living link with the golden age of the nineties. He told me that Frank Harris claimed in his youth to have been a friend of Thomas Carlyle; and that once when he had been accompanying the sage back to Jane and his Chelsea home, he had been solemnly warned by him that he must choose, like all writers, between serving God and Mammon. 'By God,' Harris cried, 'by God, Tommy, I'll do both.'

What made me doubtful of the story was the idea of anyone having the nerve to call the old dyspeptic 'Tommy'.

Henry was the only poet I had heard of to compose verses to a bloater:

The bloater in the Adriatic
Idly pursues his course erratic,
Nor dreams that fate will lead him to
The hungry poet in his attic.

And does the hungry poet think
Of bloaters at the water's brink?
Ah no, his thoughts are of the spring
And almond blossom blooming pink.

Thus never thinking of his brother
How can they hope to love each other?
He'll eat the bloater sure enough,
And you and I will eat another.

Meryl, Monica and Angela—'the ravishing Grayson girls'

The Grayson brothers: Godfrey, Brian, Tristram, Rupert and Ambrose

My sister Nancy and her husband Louis Drexel

Half the cottage had been washed away by turbulent seas; but there remained a living-room, a couple of bedrooms and a lean-to privy through which the wind whistled fiercely. From the vast expanse of beach the sea lay coiled and quivering ready for the death-spring; and the marshes of Winchelsea were waiting beyond to engulf it.

Its remoteness and isolation made it an ideal refuge for writers escaping from duns, publishers and irate females.

It had a certain rough comfort but the sea played a greater part in its life than any woman could have done; for, at certain times, the tide encroached high into the guest-chamber, so that one had to shove the bed hard against the inland wall to avoid death by drowning.

On my arrival I was greeted by Pat Kirwan, who was translating that huge and magnificent Russian novel *Women and Monks* by Josef Kallinkov, a writer of genius and probably the first of the many who have perished at Stalin's hands. With him was a fellow Irishman, Jasper Power, who was writing his most amusing novel (which we were later to publish), *Sea Green Grocer*.

Henry was on the beach inspecting the hooks of his long-lines; this he had to do continuously if he wanted to eat, because an army of cats had decided to live with him. Uninvited, they had attached themselves to him, doubtless realizing with their diabolical intuition that he would keep them in fish.

I have no particular love for cats but I was always filled with admiration when I saw the kittens swimming out to grab the best fish from the hooks before Henry could pull them in. With their rounded heads and tails rising erect from the waves, they looked like a flotilla of submarines streaking across Plymouth Sound. In consequence of this invasion of hungry homeless cats Henry wrote an excellent book on their customs and habits. In the mewing, writhing throng one stood out, a magnificent creature, obviously the senior, for he dominated the others by sheer size and dignity. I was surprised, therefore, one day, and it came as quite a shock, to see this noble animal making unmistakable sexual advances to a tomcat of far lesser charm and, I'm sure, social standing.

Later, among the weekend visitors were Gracie Fields, *chanteuse* and popular idol for whom Henry was writing a song, and Francis Winham, the property millionaire. They brought Fortnum meat products with them, a change of diet welcomed by the *literati* but not by the cats.

That night Henry must have retrieved enough fish for us to dine off the packing-case table on chairs supported by slim volumes of his poems; for afterwards well-fed we visited Francis Yeats-Brown, who had a house near Winchelsea town. I used to meet him formerly at the Bath Club where he sometimes persuaded me to play squash. He was a strange man, enormously interested in the occult and eastern lore; later he was to become well known as an editor of the *Spectator* and the author of a best-selling autobiography, *Bengal Lancer*. He interested me particularly as the product of a conventional family, with a Harrow schooling and service in a cavalry regiment, who had broken out of the mould. He had made a particular study of yoga and on one occasion he had Prince George, the Duke of Kent, standing on his head in a corner of the room for so long that Humphrey Butler, his attaché, believed his royal master had succumbed when in fact he was only in a trance.

The evening was not without its alarms. Jasper, a contemporary and close friend of Samuel Beckett at Trinity College, Dublin, was also something of a poet, specializing for some reason in Scottish ballads. The opening lines of one of them ran, I seem to remember, something like this:

Our reverend meenister
Has turned rather seenister
And taken to wearin' a beard.
While Sandy MacPherson's
Exposin' his pairson
And publicly dreein' his weird . . .

He was the son of a canon in the Church of Ireland, but apt to be violent when inebriated. Having emptied a bottle of brandy and having no further use for it, he hit Pat Kirwan with it over the head. Fortunately it was a glancing blow, but it shattered the glass of whisky in Pat's hand, and this was something no Irishman will take sitting down, so Pat stood up; and then everything happened very fast. Pat was standing up and Jasper lying down. It was one of the quickest fights I've ever seen and there was Pat neatly smoothing his hands as delicately as Turner brushing my silk hat. Yeats-Brown I could see would have liked it to have lasted longer, for he liked disputes to be settled with more ceremony, with seconds and pistols for two and coffee for one. It was all too quick for any harm to be done and, as Jasper philosophically remarked when he came to, 'What's a blow among friends?'

To vary the proceedings Francis Yeats-Brown offered to do some yoga and stood on his head in a corner. He was never without his eyeglass (I believe he slept in it) and even head down it still remained firmly screwed in its socket. Unfortunately Francis, probably owing to this sudden reversal of normal posture and the amount of drink consumed, was also sick upside down, something I had never witnessed before or, come to think of it, after.

A few hours later we were all drinking happily again at Henry's cottage, spouting verse with the cats slinking round us, the morning tide creeping into my room and a wild moon riding over the marshes.

In the 1950s Henry fell ill and was admitted to the Royal Marsden Hospital in the Fulham Road suffering from cancer of the lung. With a group of sorrowing friends we went to visit him, bearing champagne. We had quite a party; saddened only by the whispered intimation of the medico that he had but three weeks to live.

The next day, stimulated possibly by the wine, Henry leapt from his bed, dressed and caught a banana boat from the Pool of London to the Canaries, where he lived in joyful debauch for the next fifteen years. He must have been damned near 90 when he died in an old age faithfully portrayed in lines attributed to Dean Swift, but probably written by Alan Herbert or Hilaire Belloc:

From Commerce and the Busy World retir'd
Unmoved by Fame; nor by Ambition fir'd
Calmly I await the Call of Charon's Boat
Still drinking like a Fish, still fucking like a Goat.

CHAPTER VI

But wilt thou cure thine heart
of love and all its smart
Then die, dear, die.

BEDDOES

Eveleigh Nash was true to his word. In an astonishingly short time (though to me it seemed as long as the Ice Age) he had written to me accepting my book. If I'd had the sense to know it I'd conceived the idea for the hovercraft: all my excursions in the space about me were made on a cushion of air. Effortlessly I proceeded to London, assailed by congratulatory sound waves from the Winchelsea *hommes de lettres* and wails from the famished cats—while meat abounded Henry refused to fish.

I signed the contract, was given lunch at the Savoy Grill and handed a cheque for £50 advance on royalties. In my short life I had gone through thousands; but this was the first real money, apart from my pittance as a seaman, I had ever earned by ache of fingers and agonies of soul. Welsh miners, workless, were singing in the Strand; a vast depression had begun to move from the Atlantic over the heedless twenties; but I was still young and hale, a writer, and could now mix unchallenged with my peers.

While transacting my business with Eveleigh I had been introduced to Morley Roberts, a most admirable and professional artist; but one who wrote only of the things that interested him and paid no heed at all to the public's demand. He could write highly amusing stories and novels such as *The Salt of the Sea* and *The Promotion of the Admiral.* He also wrote a scholarly and affectionate account of that tragic man, George Gissing, in *The Private Life of Henry Maitland.* He had written the definitive work on his old friend, the poet-naturalist W. H. Hudson; and followed it by a volume of fishing experiences of which Rudyard Kipling had written in a letter to me: 'I like Morley's *Humble Fisherman* because he owns up to taking a delight in small trout. That's a mark of sincerity and he has a lovely touch.'

Later, the old man had come up with a book in which he recorded, after long and extensive research, philosophical and scientific, his findings on the mysterious and sinister origins of cancer. This layman's work, *Warfare in the Human Body*, was sufficiently remarkable to induce Professor Keith, then the leading authority on carcinoma, to ask if he might be allowed to write an introduction and express his admiration.

Once, visiting some rather grand acquaintances in their large country mansion (one with a long drive) Morley on arrival was joined to his surprise by a friendly little nanny goat. He rang, the butler opened the door and he was shown into a beautiful eighteenth-century drawing-room. Without hesitation the goat followed (as to the manner born, one might say) and stood ruminating by his side. Morley was soon joined by his host. Each assumed that the goat belonged to the other. Morley was a little surprised when the animal started butting the furniture and ripping the brocaded chairs with her horns; but it was no business of his to criticize the behaviour of another man's pet. On the contrary, he secretly congratulated the nanny goat on her choice of master. As she leapt from chair to chair, Morley couldn't restrain his admiration: 'How beautifully she jumps,' he said to his host. This might have continued had not the nanny goat taking advantage of Morley's host (who was bending to pick up a shattered Sèvres bowl) attacked him savagely from and in the rear. After explanations, and as no mortal wounds had been inflicted, both men parted friends. Not so, however, with a misunderstanding in which I myself played a rather 'goatish' part.

I was motoring to Scotland and had been invited to break my journey at the house of a man whom I knew only slightly. Immediately on my arrival my host explained I was to sleep in a room haunted by the ghost of a beautiful ancestress; if anything unusual occurred, would I please not mention it to his nervous but very lovely wife, to whom I could not be introduced as owing to some slight indisposition she had retired to bed.

The next morning, having breakfasted and due to depart, I was going up the grand staircase to my room to collect a few odds and ends, when, against the dim wintry light of the tall windows I saw the 'ghost' floating down towards me in the most ethereal of negligées. Elated, I whispered to her as she passed: 'What a pity you didn't come and haunt my room last night.' The 'ghost' let out a most terrestrial screech and bolted down the stairs into her husband's arms.

As sometimes happens in Scotland, it was raining heavily. I left the castle, socially and meteorologically, under a heavy cloud.

Perhaps to account for his present penury, and perhaps also to warn me against seeking money rather than indulgence of my vagrant fantasies and dreams, Morley gave me a short lecture which sometimes I wish I had heeded. 'Gaining success and acclaim in writing is like crossing a stream without getting wet,' he said. 'You pick up a stone and throw it in; then pick up another and throw that in and keep at it until you've built the stepping stones. *But you've got to throw them all in the same place.*'

The next day, my literary future assured and loaded with large tins of Cow and Gate baby food for little Antonia Drexel, I once more left London for Cannes. It was pleasant to know that I was no longer a smuggler but a bona fide traveller, carrying on my passport a special request from His Majesty's Principal Secretary of State that I should be allowed to pass 'without let or hindrance' and that anyone concerned should give me assistance and protection.

At the Calais customs with my conscience white and clear, I honourably declared all I had; it was then I realized for the first time that I was *not* going to receive the 'assistance' nor the 'protection' requested on my behalf.

I had never up to that moment, believe it or not, seen the contents of a tin of Cow and Gate. I was the possessor of ten tins of pure white powder; it looked pretty harmless to me, but to the French authorities it suggested narcotics—cocaine. They decided that every tin must be taken to a laboratory for chemical analysis. By this time the Blue Train had left and, though not under arrest, I was told I must stay under surveillance in the neighbourhood of the station. As a matter of fact this suited me admirably. Had not Edward VII, a *bon vivant* of international fame, described the seaport *restaurant de la gare* as one of the best in Europe?

Certainly I enjoyed an excellent lunch with the *Chef de Douane*, who had decided to join me, whether to entertain me or keep an eye on me I never knew nor did I care; because with a very companionable Château Margaux he kept me amused with stories of smuggling until science had declared the Cow and Gate to be innocuous and suitable only for infant consumption, and I was able to go on to Paris.

Wherever I might arrive in the world there was always a letter from Mother with news of the rest of the family or Ravenspoint, and Father, unfailingly referred to as H.M.G.—appropriate initials for someone under whose government the family thrived. I don't think we ever saw Mother idle; she was either sewing or embroidering (she had no use for knitting or crochet) or writing letters. As she grew older she would sometimes doze off after dinner (which next day she would vehemently deny) in an armchair; but it was always with her writing pad on her knees, for she never wrote at a writing table. Persuading her to go to bed was as difficult as telling a child it was bedtime. But how often those loving letters were written when she could hardly keep awake, and how often they had come to us all, scattered through the world, as rain on the desert and corn in Egypt; they were as lively as a tick of the second in the retreating moment; they were sincere and brave, but sometimes there was the distant echo of melancholy, because secretly she understood more about life's inevitable sadness than she wished us to know. She adored Father, but his frequent absences abroad and his susceptibility to other beautiful women must have hurt her deeply. She took every indiscretion and peccadillo of which he, and we, were all capable with loving understanding, accepting everything except open criticism of us. Then the tigress in her was immediately aroused because we belonged to her.

At the Hotel Danou I found a letter from her, telling me that my brother Brian had arrived back from India where he had been staying with my old school-fellow and friend of the family, Harry Elliott, whose father was the Resident in the State of Patiala. Residents in those days were very grand fellows who kept an eye on the local maharajah to see he didn't go over the budget or start any private wars.

The Maharajah of Patiala, after George V and his equerry, Harry Stonor, was considered the finest shot in the world. It appears that when he learned that the Resident had a good cricketer, bowler and fielder, as a guest in the shape of Brian, with whom he immediately made friends, he recruited him to fling ping-pong balls in the air, which he shot down unerringly with a rifle. Running short of balls and awaiting a fresh shipment, he would go off and shoot tigers from the back of an elephant, a far less exacting test of marksmanship.

The letter went on: 'Brian has arrived from India. David Tennant [the founder of the Gargoyle Club and husband of Hermione Baddeley, the slightly more beautiful of the two famous Hermiones, Baddeley and Gingold] motored him up last weekend in his enormous specially built Leyland. On the long straight stretch of road across the island he drove at 100 mph, and Brian remarked that he was rather frightened—to comfort him, I suppose, David replied: "You're not half as frightened as I am." I only hope while he's here David remembers to put lots of oil in it. . . .'

Cumberland, Mother's ex-Guardsman chauffeur who drove her Daimler, once said to her, 'The young gentlemen fill up with petrol, but they are inclined to forget the oil.' Mother had never forgotten this bit of expertise, nor were any of us allowed to forget it either. She knew nothing about cars except the purpose for which they were used; which was quite seemly. Pointing to the hand-brake and the gear-change she once asked me what the rods were for; but on the subject of lubrication she acknowledged no equal.

The letter went on to tell me that my cousin Freddie Harrington would be calling on me in Paris, whither he was proceeding in a very depressed spiritual state. Mother hoped he had no real intention of jumping, parachuteless, from the Eiffel Tower. He was suffering from a severe attack of unrequited love; which, in my experience, is really nothing more than wounded vanity, but nonetheless painful for all that.

On his arrival in Paris I strove to talk him out of his suicidal thoughts because he had alarmed me by suggesting we should go at once to the Eiffel Tower. I pointed out that it was too tasteless a structure even to end one's life from; and told him of the man who was always railing against every inch of its 990 feet. One day, a friend, ascending to the top of the tower, was amazed to find its detractor there. 'This is the last place in Paris I'd expect to see you,' said the friend. 'Yes,' said the man, 'but it's the only place in Paris I can't see it from.'

We agreed to abandon the Eiffel Tower, so I took him to have a drink at Fouquet's and endeavoured to talk him out of his intention to end it all. I quoted Shakespeare's view that men have died and worms have eaten them, but not for love. As an antidote I suggested champagne laced with brandy, quoting the example offered by Byron of 'Lord Mountcoffeehouse, the Irish peer, who killed himself for love, with wine, last year'; but Freddie would have none of it. To divert him I decided to show him the sights of Paris; the sewers, so beloved of Victor Hugo, might, as it were, bring him down to earth; and surely the enigmatic smile of the Mona Lisa would warn him of the pitfalls involved in loving only one woman at one time.

In the end there remained only the radical cure, the shock treatment : sex versus love.

I took him to 25, Porte St Denis, warning him : 'Don't tell your friends about this because it might give Paris a bad name.' I paid the hundred francs which admitted us and we proceeded to the first floor. Here, as on the four other floors, each room contained a large double bed on which a girl lay. Standing round at the bedside were those who, like us, had paid the entrance fee. It was the privilege of any spectator, if he felt so inclined, to couple with the lady on the bed in a manner of his own choosing; but not, of course, before the gentleman *in situ* had abdicated. Undressing was confined to the barest necessary so that the ensuing copulation was often all but concealed in a flurry of petticoats and overcoats. Occasionally a little comic relief was introduced, as when a pair of braces broke or a hat rolled under the bed (and had to be retrieved *à côté du pôt de chambre*) or monies spilled from trouser pockets.

This fine old house with its ten rooms, always fully occupied, was frequented mostly by voyeurs and other students of what observers describe as the Rabelaisian 'close-buttock game'. The splendid green door to the establishment opened at 2.00 p.m. and closed at the unexpectedly early hour of 6.00 p.m. (it was once explained to me that low-paid office workers were a clientèle they discouraged); the average Parisians and even the Anglo-American expatriates had never heard of the place. It is worth recording its existence because places of amusement where the visitor pays the house for the entertainment he himself provides are far from commonplace.

Freddie showed signs of interest and insisted on visiting every room so that by the time he was ready to leave the lovely old sixteenth-century house it was ready to close, so we strolled to a corner café. In our doctor-patient relationship we had come to know each other better, as people who having shared an important experience take measure of each other. I was not, therefore, altogether surprised when he asked me to take him where he could enjoy a girl's company in greater privacy.

Freddie was impecunious and could not afford the splendours of the House of All Nations, the Sphinx or the plush luxuries of the Rue Caumartin bordellos. I took him instead to a kindergarten brothel in the Rue de la Farrière, where they were unaccustomed to wealthy foreigners; and where his money would be far more appreciated by the girls serving apprenticeships there.

I arranged to meet him later at the nearby church of Notre Dame de Lorette at the foot of the hill. In the meantime I presented him to Madame. It was now 6.00 p.m. and she was at home to her clients, with her young assistants, intent on amassing a dowry and a husband, awaiting with docility the summons to the selection parade. To distinguish one novice from the other—for they were remarkably alike, being often recruited from the same family—each wore in her hair a beautifully ironed ribbon, all of varying hue, tied neatly in a bow.

After the sordid communal activities of the Porte St Denis establishment it was pleasing to leave him in this friendly atmosphere of starched petticoats and freshly laundered sheets. An hour later in the whispering silence and aromatic twilight of the old church I suddenly realized that he was kneeling beside me, and in that moment I felt closer to him than I had been all day. Freddie was cured and offering up his thanks to a kindly and all-forgiving God.

Next morning fate guided my drifting footsteps into the Scribe to find out whether my old friend Duncan Orr-Lewis, a director of the hotel, was in Paris. He was not, but his brother-in-law, Sir

Albert Stern, was. Over a drink in the bar he asked me what my plans were. I have noticed through a long life that people have always been interested in my plans: as though I, of all people, was the type of man who knew what he would be doing in any twenty-four hours ahead. I told him, on the spur of the moment, I had a great longing to visit Bucharest. 'Why not go on one of my tankers as my guest,' he said to my surprise. 'From Constanza you can take a train to Bucharest.'

There are times when life takes you by the throat and throws you into the scuppers and other times when it embraces you as a loved one and treats you as part of the establishment, someone to be petted and protected. To have refused Sir Albert's invitation would have been foolish and ungrateful, so I accepted promptly. The sailing date from the United Kingdom just gave me time to deliver my precious cargo of Cow and Gate; so it was in a very amiable mood that I boarded the Blue Train for Cannes.

I unrolled my small royal Bokhara on the floor of my wagon-lit. It was one of my remaining possessions and a beloved one; I was never so content as when I felt its sleeky pile under my bare feet in the cool morning or unfriendly night.

Travelling overland has for me a strange fascination. The life of a train is like that of a moving hotel: bars and restaurants, sleeping quarters, well-stocked fridges, wine lockers and linen cupboards; kitchens and resident servants, day-and-night life, all traversing the fair land of France. In the deep night the train pulled up. Rain must have fallen because the moonlight disclosed a glistening line of poplars aspiring to the stars; and in the silence that followed the groaning and grinding of brakes I was conscious of the train breathing like a living thing.

CHAPTER V

I must go down to the sea again,
to the vagrant gipsy life.

MASEFIELD

What a lass that were to go
a-gipsying through the world with.

LAMB

A week later I joined the tanker *Staua Romana* at Thames Haven as supercargo—the only passenger on a commercial vessel: this became a way of life that, intermittently, I was to follow for many years. Once more I was to stand on a ship's deck, spellbound, with the immense breathing ocean stretching to the horizon; beyond lay fresh worlds of mystery and adventure. I was in thrall to romantic names.

I had already sailed the Spanish Main, rolled down to Rio and the River Plate. I had been through the Panama Canal into the Pacific, sailed north to Yokohama and south to Guayaquil, Callao and Valparaiso, blessed city where my mother was born. I knew Canada and the United States, the Gulf ports and the Pacific coast to Long Beach, that brash port for Los Angeles, and on to San Francisco. I knew most of the European capitals and Leningrad and Moscow; but I longed for the golden cities of the Orient; their gateways were Istanbul by sea and Bucharest overland. I had been told that Bucharest had everything that makes a city agreeable: beautiful women, night-smelling flowers, scented wine and flowing music. Besides all this I liked the sound of the name. It had the softness and the crispness of a croissant straight from the oven.

We sailed on the evening tide. The captain was a Rumanian from the Danubian basin. Like most foreign ships' masters, he had a working knowledge of English, and in better French he revealed a puckish humour.

We lived in a style at that time unheard of in a British tanker. A varied menu of Rumanian dishes with a splendid rough wine was served at every meal, preceded by Suica, an insidious aperitif which soon ingratiated itself into my affection, just as Pisco had done in Peru.

Some of the meals I wouldn't have exchanged for dinner at the Tour d'Argent. My own quarters had a bunk as narrow as a monk's bed, a washbasin and one port; but there was a bathroom, a luxury to which, as an old deckhand, I was quite unused.

I tried to regulate work on my new book by the watches kept by the deck and engine-room officers. The Chief Officer, who did the four to eight watch, was an enormous man with all the good nature that one associates (sometimes wrongly) with a fat man. He caused amusement at meals because he unfortunately suffered from *gannetitis*: like the gannet he tried to put more into his mouth than the orifice allowed. But he was a particularly talented carpenter, and it was fascinating watching him making toys for his children; these he tinted with vegetable dyes—the bright reds, blues, yellows and greens of the peasant. As he carved and painted them it reminded me of the late Lord Howard de Walden: no one knew more about toys. In childhood Tommy's impecunious parents had only been able to give him the cheapest toys and in this deprived condition he had remained until his 21st birthday, when the holder of the barony most suddenly died. At that moment Tommy became of age, inherited the title and all the monies accruing from the vast estates. From being poor he became one of the wealthiest men in England.

All this happened just before the turn of the century when the Government and my dear friend Rudyard Kipling were calling for volunteers to go and fight the Boers. Tommy had just enlisted in the Yeomanry, and now as Trooper Lord Howard de Walden was on embarkation leave.

He sped at once to Hamley's toy shop, then in Oxford Street, and bought up the store. He played all night with them (these toys that in childhood he had only dreamed of); then shipped the whole lot off next morning to the Children's Hospital in Great Ormond Street.

He then called at the bank, drew out £1,000 in gold sovereigns, took the money in a chamois-leather bag aboard the troopship and handed it around as the fancy took him.

He never outgrew his delight in toys. At Chirk Castle he had a model harbour built in the grounds, an artificial lake complete with every kind of installation, all electrically controlled: loading and unloading berths, sheds, railways on the quayside and cranes with ships to scale of every kind. I used to watch him with Rudyard Kipling, both bending over their toys, for all the world like two boys, save for the twin bald heads reflected in the lake.

One evening at Chirk Castle, drawn by the distant notes, I groped my way through long corridors lit only by the occasional glint of moonlight on armour, until I at last found the ancient hall where Tommy had installed a full-sized organ, a mighty Wurlitzer; and I stood in the shadows until the last note in the finale echoed through the rafters. He was playing a romantic opera he had composed called *Bronwen* which, though it had been performed with an amateur cast, had never been produced professionally. I asked him why he had not put it on himself. 'If no one's prepared to risk their money, why should I risk mine?' he replied; unlike Sydney Beer, who came of a wealthy family of Liverpool cotton brokers and had musical aspirations. Sydney had no hesitation in hiring the London Symphony Orchestra to accompany his conducting at the Albert Hall; which they did with great skill and secret amusement.

The captain of the *Staua Romana* needed no help in the making of music. One evening, when we were clear of the Channel, he produced a violin case. I was immediately visited by that nervous tension felt by most Englishmen at the appearance of this instrument. It is not altogether surprising the Roman populace were astonished when Nero started fiddling while their city was burning to the ground. Well they might be, particularly as the violin was not invented until two centuries later; he must have surely mislaid his lute. I had learned during school days the torture of an indifferently played violin, so painful as to become in time a sado-masochistic bond between executant and auditor. It has been said that in totalitarian countries the police interrogator and his victim become complementary, each so dependent on the other that separation becomes as unbearable to the tortured as it does to the torturer; an uneasy relationship not unlike that of the lion and his tamer, bound in unity by the lash.

I am ashamed to say, therefore, that it was with these emotions that I watched the captain cradle his fiddle in his arms and tuck it lovingly beneath his chin: as his guest I immediately assumed, to the best of my ability, an expression of happy anticipation. What wonderful surprises life can sometimes hold in store for the young (who believe they know everything); for that evening, quite undeservedly, I was privileged to hear the most exquisite and exciting succession of gipsy melodies played with a verve unequalled in all my experience. The captain treated his fiddle as a loved one, petting and stroking it, coaxing it and sometimes, it seemed, punishing it. I hadn't sufficient knowledge to judge technique; but the feeling and passion, the laughter and tears he drew from his beloved instrument was overwhelming. I had not enjoyed music so wild and singing since Kreisler once played to me alone in his suite at the Hyde Park Hotel.

When the captain realized how I enjoyed his music he played every night, and I believe he liked to think he inspired me at my work, writing, a poor thing compared to his music.

A few nights later the escalating lights of Gibraltar showed up on our port bow and next day the cork forests and the mountains of Andalucia's Costa del Sol stretched north-eastwards, culminating in the white peaks of the Sierra Nevada.

A week later off Cape Matapan, the most southerly point in Greece, the ship's whistle blew, the engines stopped. Soon a small boat put off from the rocky mainland. As it came alongside, leaning over the rail with the chief engineer, I watched stores being lowered to an old white-bearded man who stacked them carefully on the floorboards of his frail craft. I was told that he had lost his ship, his wife, his crew and all he had in the world when his ship went ashore on that merciless coast. Since then he had lived in a cave on a ledge of rock, existing on the stores left by friendly passing ships. There are certain pictures which remain fixed in the mind's eye; the old man pulling away from the ship's side, his farewell wave of the arm and his long white beard parted by the wind is one of them.

We crossed the Aegean Sea with the gulls breasting the wind and escorting the ship in sweeping circles. The isles of Greece surrounded us on all sides in jagged silhouette, rising in the afterglow of the sunset black as ebony from the deeps and the shallows. As twilight drifted into darkness the stars came out and the silver web of the Milky Way spread itself above Skyros and Missalonghi, where my fellow Harrovian died bedridden of a fever, instead of heroically on the battlefield as he would have wished.

Father had warned me that Istanbul was beautiful only when seen from the deck of a ship. Seen from our anchorage the violet-crowned city rested luminously in the sunrise on its seven hills, the mosques and minarets floating in the rosy and golden haze. When I went ashore I was quickly swallowed in a squalid maze of rutted streets and alleys deep in filth and refuse of a most disagreeable kind.

I did the rounds of the bazaars and St Sophia, the church of Holy Wisdom, with its fantastic acoustics and superb mosaics. I wandered through the shadows of the gardens of the Topkapi Palace, the old Seraglio of the Sultans. It was here that the last sultan, Abdul Hamid, had garrotted over 2,000 concubines, presumably in defence of what little energies they had left him. The air was charged with the stale smell and the bitter taste of cruelty, torture and death; I sensed that same unmistakable, indescribable evil was there as it had been in the underground cells of the Fortress of Peter and Paul in Leningrad.

I hurried back to the streets searching vainly for the romantic, exotic city of Pierre Loti. At every corner I encountered those malignant and secret smells so familiar to me, the accumulation of hundreds of years of filth and dirt which instinctively came alive and crept forward at my approach as if to salute me as an old friend. The wider streets were teeming with ill-humoured crowds who pushed and, worse, nudged from all sides. They moved like ants mysteriously about their business, but there were others with obvious purpose who bashed their way on to the overloaded trams and swarmed down to the Scutari ferry boats. Once I saw a flower-laden girl with the Orient in her eyes. She was unveiled and walked like a princess across the Galata Bridge; in the throng she seemed to tread a solitary path that opened at her approach; it was as pleasing and unexpected as the sight of a rose on a dungheap.

At one time in my wanderings I sensed I was being stalked by a yellow cur, for there were plenty of lean dogs with ancestral memories prowling the city and the edge of the waters searching, as their fathers did in Byron's day, for the headless trunks flung there from the Sultan's palace. The horrible animals seemed to be everywhere. I was told they rarely left their own section of the city, for if a dog wandered out of his own particular territory he was at once set upon and torn asunder; when they moved into alien land it was only in packs, like the street gangs in New York.

I was meeting the captain later for dinner, so early in the evening I called on one of Father's shipowner friends. He was a widower and I had been told lived alone: if he did it was with a garland of rosy-lipped Georgian boys who greeted me with sweet smiles. His gloomy old palace was furnished in faded Victorian splendour; heavily curtained, silver and crystal ornaments everywhere, and each room choc-a-bloc with little tables and drowsy divans, against a background of columns supporting phallic arches. The ceilings were studded with gold and silver crescents and stars, the Kula and Bergama carpets and rugs I'd never seen before were magnificent. His knowledge of England was confined to the Cecil Hotel, Billiter Street, St Mary Axe and a visit paid in the nineties to Hastings.

I was offered little cakes, a choice of rose-leaf or orange-blossom jam and a sweet liquor not to my liking. In the garden which overhung the Bosphorus, two or three ancient gardeners were working. 'These Bulgarians know more about flowers and trees than any other Europeans,' he said, as though it were necessary to excuse their presence in this place so clearly dedicated to youth. Before I left he gave me a box of ten-inch-long cigarettes with gold scissors to cut them to the required length. As I left the palace a merciful twilight had fallen on the city and the muezzins were calling the faithful to prayer.

I met my captain at the Pera Palace Hotel, a famous caravanserai of that period. I soon learned that besides being a skilled ship's master and a brilliant violinist he was a pleasure-loving man, a *coureur de nuit* at whose approach the bright lights flashed a welcome. After dinner we drove to a house off the Rue de Pera where we drank *şarap* with a bevy of Armenian and Circassian girls. They danced a Turkish version of the Nautch with arms and hands undulating, hips swaying, bellies rolling and feet motionless. A heavily made-up boy coaxed sounds from a strange mediaeval instrument. According to custom, from our elevated positions on a mountain of rugs and cushions we showered them with silver coins, which they pressed to their foreheads where miraculously they stayed; soon we became aware of a sense of suppressed excitement among the dancers but surprisingly as the tempo of the music grew so the movements of the slim, musky, hairless bodies slowed, until they stilled into a sensual drowsiness; and one little dancer followed the other like petals falling from a dusky flower on to the foothill rugs at our feet.

As the candles burned down I lost all contact with my brave captain, nor did I know in the dream-like confusions of slender arms and budding breasts and kissing tongues which girl's mouth was breathing jasmine into mine or which was whispering in an alien tongue into my ear. They disrobed us with cool hands, playing and squabbling over us like children with their dolls and chattering unintelligible endearments: then the music faded away in a dying orgiastic moan.

Outside our old *cocher* waited with oriental patience to drive us home to our ship.

As I disembarked at Constanta en route to Bucharest the Captain played me ashore with a *tzigane* lament that held me in its melancholy thrall until I began to near that destination so long desired. Bucharest still had its orchards and every square its trees. Unexpectedly at every turning one encountered the smell of meadows, the tang of drying hay and the homely stench of the farmyard. It was impossible not to sense the slovenly Turkish influence dragging the city to the brink of disenchantment, but never quite over it. For me it had the charm of a superbly beautiful slut.

On arriving in any strange city, I always go straightaway to the leading hotel; rather as one breaks the crust of a pie before getting down to the meat inside. So I had, as the French insist, 'descended' at the Hotel Pallas Athene. This was a sort of Ruritanian Ritz-Carlton with a pleasing Edwardian atmosphere, reflecting in its diamond-studded mirrors the café society of Bucharest at every angle as they strolled and drank and flirted under the glittering crystal chandeliers. It was not without a raffish charm of a rather high order, particularly at night, when the women were dressed *haute toilette* and the men were wearing glittering decorations and medals to which they were probably not entitled.

Any traveller knows that for sociability and good manners he must find his way to the bar; for this is the pulse of the hotel. Apart from being the source of information and gossip, it is here that people control their likes and dislikes and discipline themselves to a mood of careless affability, thus creating an atmosphere most agreeable for the lonely wanderer; but it takes more than a few potato crisps and a brass footrail to make a bar—it needs the barman. At the Pallas Athene the bar was the favourite rendezvous of the Government officials, whose negative attitude to uncongenial labours exceeded even my own; the younger secretaries and attachés of the Diplomatic Corps; the painted, powdered and corseted army officers, the *demi-mondaines*, the foreign correspondents and the inevitable lean and hungry men and women who live by the sale of negotiable information or the cupidity and indiscretions of the wealthy. At this cosmopolitan meeting place at 6.30 every evening (the only punctuality observed in Bucharest) the curtain rose on the Balkan scene to the distant strains of a pale-blue-uniformed Hungarian orchestra playing *Les Millions d'Harlequin*, *The Blue Danube* or *Un Peu d'Amour*.

Soon I was meeting men with vaguely official jobs who had no difficulty in persuading me to adopt their custom of driving round the city in an open *drozhki* driven by peak-capped coachmen in velvet kaftans, visiting bars, cafés and cat-houses; and ending up at midnight in one of the many summer restaurants, where we listened to gipsy music, ate fresh caviar, chicken cooked in sour cream or veal with tomato sauce and paprika, drinking Copner or another red wine I like enormously called Dragasani to which they had thoughtfully introduced me. Needless to say I was completely enchanted with the wild, singing music of the *tziganes*: and I found the Balkan gipsy far more appealing than the fawning and touching fingers of the *gitanos* of Granada and Seville.

Bertie Stern had given me several letters of introduction, but I knew that if they were the people I'd wish to meet in a small capital like Bucharest I would, in course of time, meet them in any event. Nor did I like the feeling that letters of introduction (and even letters of recommendation) placed the recipients under an obligation to entertain, however boring they might find you; but some years later I used one quite happily. It was to Sir William Wiseman, in New York, a partner in the well-known Wall Street brokers, Kahn Loeb. I was staying at the St Moritz on 69th Street, in a room with a glorious view over Central Park. As a faithful European I had chosen it because of its name and because it had a Rumpelmeyer's on the ground floor, though I learned later it had no association with that most delicious of all *pâtisseries* in the Rue de Rivoli. One morning of a lovely Indian summer's day, fortified with a dry martini, adorned with a carnation and armed with an umbrella, I set off on foot downtown. I intended handing in my letter of introduction and leaving a card with my address; and then taking a look at that section of New York where the tycoons operated, those business millionaires who did the wisest things by day and the silliest things at night. By the time I reached Fourth Avenue (where my publishers, the charming MacRea brothers of E. P. Dutton, had their offices) I was quite exhausted, and I finished the journey on the subway emerging at Wall Street rather relieved to escape, because the sight of an Englishman's umbrella and his buttonhole was still a source of mild amusement to the natives.

At the very grand offices in William Street I handed my letter to a very grand porter; but I was taken by surprise when he asked me to wait in case there was a reply. A few minutes later I was ushered into the presence of Sir William Wiseman. For a young man this was both unexpected and a little alarming. I had supposed that in due course I might be invited to his home to sample a cocktail; but to be received immediately was like a junior clerk being summoned to the boardroom of Rothschild's.

Sir William was an Englishman who had lived in America for many years and was both liked and respected. He had been a close friend of President Wilson during the First World War, in which he had served our Secret Service with great astuteness. Besides being a high-calibre tycoon he was a man of impeccable taste in all things worldly, adorning his home with the loveliest of the Ziegfield Folly girls, whom he married at the short but legally necessary intervals.

He at once introduced me to Otto Kahn, the multi-multi-millionaire, who had a desk in the same room. Kahn, as if to take the curse off his vast business ramifications, was a man of erudition and culture. He was the chief backer of the Metropolitan Opera House, a patron of the arts; and a collector of old masters rather than young mistresses.

It was nearing luncheon time, and I was straight away invited to the Bankers' Club. Here at the bar we were served jumbo dry martinis from their private jug, but I was offered no wine at the table. Their conversation gave no clue to how this English tenth baronet and his cultured Jewish partner had been drawn together in a country alien to them both, in which it was still fondly and wrongly believed there were no social barriers or limits to ambitions. The answer might lie in my own experience. Here was I, a young man, being entertained by two of the leading men on Wall Street with no recommendation except a letter. This could only happen in America, where the colonial tradition of hospitality persists.

It is true that the letter had described me as a writer; and even though writers are two a dime, there exists in America a mystical respect for the written word and for anyone who had produced a book. Most men, however much experience of life they have had, feel somehow incomplete unless they can commit it to paper. Both my hosts had, of course, recounted their life-stories in countless balance-sheets, and I suspected an interest in me which would have quickly evaporated if they had sent to E. P. Dutton for the sales figures of my latest book.

With these two brilliant men of finance I was navigating in shallow waters. They were polite enough to encourage me to speak of myself, a subject on which I had every reason to be reticent, so (artfully, I hope) I steered the conversation into other channels. Of one thing I was certain: they were treating me with more courtesy than I deserved; and I was grateful. There was only one moment when I felt a little alarmed, when I believed they were about to suggest a regular job; but as the luncheon went on they must have realized that I had no intention of working my fingers to the bone in America or anywhere else. However, I had met two men who were to befriend me for many years in frequent later visits to New York.

So too in Bucharest, the British Minister, Edward Greig, and his wife were delightful; and the legation, a small but charming house set in its own garden, was singularly free from the Office-of-Works monotony that permeates so many embassies and legations: *entrance hall, chandelier, crystal, one for the use of.*

I already knew there was more to be learned from someone by introducing the subject in which he was most interested, be it about the man himself. I can truthfully say I was by now an accomplished listener, even if I was never to learn a methodical system of filing the knowledge I acquired. I was also learning to be an observer—I noticed what men, and particularly women, wore and this would sometimes give me an insight into their characters. A neat dresser usually had a neat mind, a careless dresser a careless mind—the snags were the exceptions. Father used to say, 'When you meet someone, man or woman, however colourless, there's always one big thing in their lives which is important to them. Find out what it is and you've made a friend.' Yet, in spite of this I missed, more often than not, important or amusing points of contact. On my return to London I had looked up Greig in *Who's Who* and learned that he had been at my preparatory school, Bilton Grange; this would have created a common interest, but unfortunately I had sadly failed to discuss the full range of his life.

Many years later, when I was staying in Ipswich at the White Hart (advertised rather coyly as a 'Dickens hotel') I met a delightful American in the bar and we decided to dine together before he caught the London train. Over dinner we discussed cabbages and kings, for he was well read and a man of varied interests.

Before he left to catch his train he said, 'I hope we meet again. My name's Sikorski.'

'What, the helicopter man?' I asked.

'That's me,' he replied as he leapt into his taxi. *Me miserum!* I'd missed hearing an expert talking on his own subject. Nor will I ever forgive myself over the infuriating lapse with Berry Wall, an American expatriate living in Paris. Often we used to walk in the Avenue Bois de Boulogne when he was exercising his two chows; as well known to Parisians of that period as the Dolly Sisters, who were both reported to be kept by Selfridge, who had a store in Oxford Street; and he would talk of most things but I never learned that he was a close friend of Marcel Proust. When we parted he must have often been on his way to that dimly-lit, over-heated, cork-lined room at the Ritz where the great writer had insulated himself from the outside world. Berry was a kind man and I feel sure he would have taken me into that unholy of holies.

In Ipswich that night Sikorski and I had dined early, so I went alone rather disconsolately to the local cinema. Even through half-closed, sleepy eyes I realized the picture was about to reach its climax when suddenly the film broke and the urgent summons was flashed on the screen: WILL DOCTOR RUPERT GRAYSON GO IMMEDIATELY TO THE WHITE HART HOTEL. At the hotel I found a rather tipsy Tiny Campbell. He was the only page of honour at George V's coronation who later became an innkeeper; and, as one would expect, a very charming one. He was an old friend. Learning I was staying at the hotel, he had used his ingenuity to such good purpose and with such confidence that a pint of beer was waiting for me on the bar.

'Sorry to call you out on a night like this,' he said in his shameless way. 'What's on the operating table for tonight, Doctor?'

Next to innkeepers and barmen, the most interesting and tricky body of men whose vocation it is to aid and instruct the traveller I have found to be chauffeurs, *cochers*, gondolieri and rickshaw boys; so I took an immediate interest in the Bucharest *skapelz*. They were their own masters, drove *drozhkis* in the summer and sleighs in the winter, and being persecuted for their religious beliefs had fled from Russia in the last century. They married early, and after producing a couple of children submitted themselves to a radical castration: hence their girth and placidity. I was young then, and can truthfully state that at no time in my life had I ever even toyed, as they say, with the idea of castration. Indeed it filled me, as I sat behind a *skapelz* and viewed his vast buttocks, with horror and dismay; but now, advanced in years and with the population explosion frighteningly upon us, I see these men as pioneers pointing mankind to its only means of survival and salvation.

Although *steatopygia* in the case of the Bucharest *skapelz* can hardly be looked on as contributing in any way to beauty in the male, these amplitudes in women are spoken of most highly by serious students of the female form. Frank Budgen, the painter-poet (whom Pat Kirwan and I persuaded to write that model source-book, *James Joyce and the Making of Ulysses*) tells a story of the Irish master's interest in the feminine B.T.M. He told of an African monarch whose method of selecting his annual tribute of wives had an endearing simplicity, amounting almost to genius.

Two posts were erected before the royal throne with a raffia rope stretched tautly between them; and before this the prospective topless brides were ranged in line abreast. At a blast from the Master of Ceremonies on a hollowed elephant tusk and to the music of flutes, the beauties backed down to the raffia rope until it touched their rears and a blast from the elephant tusk halted them.

Then, *feierlich*, as the Germans say, with dignity and ceremony, the monarch rose and proceeded to the poles where the royal eye looked down the rope and the contiguous bums. Thus could exact comparison be made and exact judgement of curve, magnitude and distance from ground level. 'It is to be hoped,' Joyce would conclude, 'that it was given to this enlightened potentate to reign over his people for many, many happy years.'

The *skapelz* drove coal-black horses of the famous Imperial Orloff blood. I had first seen these castrati looming bulky and upright on the *drozhkis* when we had driven out to the *gradinas* (the garden restaurants), but as they came down from the driving-seat and stood by their animals I saw in the bulk of their bodies a plumpness and hairlessness, making them look half-woman, half-man. They were looked on as men of discretion who could be entrusted with confidential errands, and had in fact established themselves in their honourable calling much as the London hansom-cab drivers had done in the Edwardian era.

After a few days I found myself becoming too involved with the habitués of the Pallas Athene, so I moved to the Grand Hotel, an unpretentious place in spite of its name. It was well managed, surprisingly, by an Englishman, confounding the generally accepted view that a successful hotel must have a Swiss manager, a French chef and pastry-cook, Italian waiters, a German hall porter, a Bulgarian gardener; and an Englishman in the car park. This expatriate with his frockcoat, striped trousers and diplomatic address would have graced any embassy. On the ground floor the hotel was run with the utmost decorum; but in the rooms and corridors above, dark-eyed, laughing maids dressed in vivid peasant costume played a variety of bedmaking, dusting and sweeping games which included an alarming belly dive down the stairs on one of the blue and red Altanian rugs.

A Frenchman who had come up to my room for a drink was so enchanted with one of these girls that he at once made overtures to her of an unmistakable character. She was obviously not unwilling; but as none of us had a common language it was difficult for her to explain that at the moment it was not, for feminine reasons, possible, so carefully choosing a carnation from a bowl of multi-coloured blooms that stood on my bedside table, she lifted her skirt above voluminous white bloomers and held the scarlet flower against her thigh. Her dark eyes were impudent and laughing but the gesture was simple, affectionate and completely informative.

The Rumanian Minister in London, M. Titulescu, had given me a letter of introduction to M. Duca, the Minister of Foreign Affairs. Obligingly he countersigned the visa on my passport in his own hand; and I was later told that thus armed I could now commit any normal non-political crime without police interference. In many ways Rumania was like other oriental and semi-oriental countries. You could do the wrong things if you knew the right people, and as in the United States, where a change of government means a change of road-sweepers, it was prudent to be politically far-sighted. In the nick of time, as it proved, I was shown the Arc de Triomphe, erected at vast expense to commemorate the allies' victory in the Great War and now about to be unveiled. This marmoreal structure was similar in design to the famous Arc in Paris. At the base were two large lions *couchant* guarding the great arch with heraldic disdain.

At the opening ceremony a quarrel broke out between the president of the reception committee and the architect, who announced with bitterness to the distinguished gathering, in the hearing of the assembled multitude, that he had not yet been paid for his services. The climax of the angry scuffle into which the quarrel developed was reached when the architect delivered a crafty blow with his umbrella at the nearest lion, instantly decapitating it and sending the shattered head rolling down the ceremonial carpet.

In the tense silence that followed, it was suddenly realized that the noble marble was of nothing more than grade-two plaster.

A spontaneous roar of Rumanian laughter burst from the delighted citizens.

I had been invited to watch the military parade from the palace of one of those charming, dark-eyed Rumanian princesses of which there seemed to be a delightful abundance.

Our view was balcony-high and from it could be seen the full length of the street and the square to which columns of soldiers were proceeding. Behind us, in the drawing-room, there was an even braver sight, far more to my taste, a long line of bottles of Rumanian wine from every province, ice-cold and redolent of wild flowers; there was unlimited *Zakuski*, cold or hot, with the exciting fragrance that comes only from dishes cooked on gipsy fires.

I had naturally simulated enthusiasm at the parade which was snaking its perspiring way below us, but, to be truthful, all military parades, displays, tattoos, and tournaments are alien to my nature, nor do I care for martial music, however well played. On this occasion it was the military bands who stole the show. I cannot recount the monstrous events from their beginning, as I had been with my hostess in the drawing-room; but when we emerged on to the balcony we were met with a din completely beyond my skill to describe.

Apparently some sort of traffic dislocation had caused the head of the column to halt at the opening of the square overlooked by our balcony. The word of command, if there had been one, could not have penetrated further than this leading column, because the next advancing column was overflowing into it, spreading itself like water, and finding its own level wherever it could or would.

At first, with splendid presence of mind, the original military band played on, determined to allay any possible panic—the show must go on. But it carried on, unfortunately, with what can only be described as obstinacy; for now the second band, in the natural order of events, appeared on the scene.

A kind of monstrous military-band contest ensued; neither body of musicians would give way to the other and the consequent clamour and noise, as the rich English say, buggered description.

Never had I, nor surely any of the party, heard so strange, so strident and so chaotic a blend of sounds until, to our stunned amazement, a third band, blaring away and with colours flying, bore into sight and flung itself into the fray. Each band, now in full blast, endeavoured to outblow, outpipe, outcymbal, outdrum and even outwit the others by infiltrating fifth columnists into each of their rival ranks. In the general confusion and cacophony I stood transfixed, glass in hand, awed by the certainty that I was hearing the very screams and clamour that must have heralded all the births of mankind.

However formal an occasion, none seemed without a certain informality. At Capsa, the city's leading restaurant, I was returning hospitality to friends. In the centre of the magnificent entrance a pail of dirty water had been inadvertently left; this, without comment, my guests semi-circumnavigated. Outside, one of the sentries guarding the Royal Palace had a bright flower blooming from the barrel of his rifle; and even at Mass I heard Viennese waltzes drifting downstream on the distant Danube.

Had I not still loved Paris, I might have succumbed to Bucharest, feminine, languorous and deceitful. I suppose I should have visited the museums and inspected the historical monuments; and feasted my eyes on the El Grecos hanging in exile in the royal palaces. Instead I had devoted my time to the ridiculous and, at moments, to the sublime.

Inevitably twilight drifted in on my last evening and the stars came out over the city. With a party of my friends we drove behind a pair of magnificent Orloffs to a *gradina* on the Sinaia road where we drank large quantities of chilled wine. As always we were entertained by the *tziganes*, encouraging them with endless toasts to even wilder music until shattered glasses surrounded us like a glittering arctic sea. Though there were Contacozinis, Ghykis, Esterhazys, Bratianos and Bibescos in our party, the gipsies, as usual, showed utter disregard for rank or wealth, addressing all by Christian name. They introduced my name into their music and drank my health in song. The entire assembly, gipsy girls and Rumanian aristocrats, joined in the singing. Not since childhood when we danced the party game of 'Who'll come gathering nuts in May' had I heard my name in song, so now in this little garden restaurant it was very pleasing to hear it pronounced in a dozen different ways. Occasionally a gipsy, overcome with fatigue and alcohol, would slide quietly to the ground; and one of the children would pick up the fiddle and continue the *czardias* where he had left off. It was *my* night;

so I was seated in the place of honour with the splendid privilege of keeping the wine flowing.

Then a dark-eyed gipsy, slim as a fairy-tale goosegirl, came to the table. Unlike the others she was in black, except for the scarlet belt entwined with yellow and purple ribbons round her waist. I was wearing a loose white blouse I had bought in Russia, fitting closely round the neck and buttoning across the shoulder; and through its fine cotton when I held her hand I could feel the warmth of her body, the impulsive pressure of her fingers and the sharp points of her copper bracelets pricking into me. Standing beside me she sang songs (very wicked ones I was told) with a voice as pure and harmonious as a choirboy's.

It was a night memorable for me for the gay company, the music and the dancing, the white light of the moon and the magical shadows cast by the trees; and because it was the first time I had experienced the sharp, wild smell of a gipsy girl in my arms.

CHAPTER VI

As I walk along the Bois du Bou-long
With an independent air
I hear the girls declare
He must be a million-aire
He's the Man who Broke the Bank at Monte Carlo.

MUSIC HALL DITTY

I had meant to go back to England in the *Staua Romana*, but I'd only been in Bucharest a few hours before I was handed a cable from Duncan Orr-Lewis asking me to meet him at the Avia Palace in Lisbon. As my trip to Rumania had been arranged through his brother-in-law, Bertie Stern, I felt that *par politesse* I should agree.

The journey by rail across Europe was not without its complications as I had to change trains at Belgrade, Trieste, Venice and Genoa; but I was on my home ground on the stretch from Ventemille to Marseilles. I knew every tunnel and every curve, where the line divided the sea and the rose-red rocks along to St Raphael where we turned inland. The familiar stuffy smell of the wagon-lit was only relieved by little winds off the sea or rural odours whenever the train halted.

I knew that Duncan would not have cabled me if it hadn't seemed important at the time; but he usually acted on impulse, and always generously. The money bags that burdened him were inherited; so they left no chips as on the sensitive shoulders of some of my friends who had had to work for them. Duncan was one of the expert Bentley and Bugatti boys, an A-class skier, a Cresta rider, a scratch golfer, a first-class helmsman and damned good-looking. I don't believe he liked cricket: except when watching it from the Tavern at Lord's where we would meet during an Eton and Harrow match, he wearing his red carnation in contest with my cornflower of blue. In the cable he asked me to wait in Lisbon until he showed up on his yacht *Volonté*.

On arrival at the Avia Palace I found a large sum of money in escudos deposited in our joint names. Duncan had a well-trained firm of accountants who were experts in legitimately transferring monies; those were the days before the imposition of Treasury control, when people were still allowed to spend or invest their money in whatever and wherever they wished. In fact, their money (strange though it may now seem) belonged to them.

I waited for Duncan for over a week, spending days in Estoril, then uninfested by royal refugees; but I had to keep in touch with the hotel in case Duncan suddenly arrived, intending to sail on the next tide. The hotel in the long Avenida de Mayo was one of the smallest and most beautiful hotels in Europe. Calouste Gulbenkian, the father of my old Harrow friend, Nubar, lived there; and when one lunched or dined there he was to be seen towering at a table placed high on a dais. As the world knows, Gulbenkian as a young man had charmed the oil company for whom he acted as middleman in securing concessions into paying him five per cent in perpetuity on oil concessions. This had made him a man of fantastic wealth, and now from his elevated position in the restaurant he was able to observe everyone, but, like the bird-watcher, it was himself (*rara avis*) who came under the closer observation.

Already in these few days I loved this capital so royal, even though the kings and captains had long departed. I first met Dom Manuel, the last king, in Munich where I had sat next to him at a cycle of Wagner's *Ring*, where he followed each opera from a dog-eared score. For a romantic like myself to meet the last of the Bourbons against this sonorous background was quite an experience.

Later I used to meet him in Cannes where he played chemin de fer for reasonably high stakes, 'banco-seuling' from table to table rather than sitting down to gamble; but I never saw him at the big table, then so successfully run by the Greek syndicate. In England he often invited me to his house, Fulwell Park. Once when I'd taken my impecunious uncle Maurice there for luncheon one of the royal servants removed an emergency £10 note which he kept sewn in his overcoat lining.

At the age of 17 Manuel became King of Portugal, where a revolution was already overdue. It was later precipitated by a visit to Paris and a brief but fateful love affair with Gaby Delys, a beautiful dancer and *chanteuse* from the Midi. The 'royal romance' established the little *artiste* but helped lose the monarch his throne. The revolutionary party started a rumour that the King had given Gaby a generous helping of the famous Braganza crown jewels. Early one morning in 1907, the King and his English mother, Queen Amelie, had to flee the palace and eventually boarded a British destroyer to seek refuge in England.

Like the post-Napoleonic Orléans family he chose to settle in Twickenham. In later exile Manuel was walking the terrace at Monte Carlo, when he noticed a man of considerable (and proletarian) poundage lifting his hat to him. The King stopped and asked: 'Your appearance is familiar, sir. Where have we met?'

'We have never met formally your Majesty, but I am the publican from Twickenham where I keep The Crown.'

Ruefully the ex-King replied: 'That's more than I could do.'

Manuel had the finest library of old Portuguese books in existence. On his death he left it to the nation which had banished him.

Leslie Bawden Allen, manager of Morgan Hargies, the bankers, in the Place Vendôme, told me a story about Gaby Delys. It appeared that the bank, in a careless moment, had advanced a large sum of money to a man in South Africa, accepting as security an ostrich farm. Steadily the farm lost money and the bank realized they were unlikely to recover their loan. Should they foreclose, it meant they would be landed with many thousands of ostriches but no cash. The bank, despite its vast ramifications and sensitivity to the slightest movement in world markets, knew nothing of ostriches, except that when nervous they stuck their heads in sand; they were, in three words, at a loss. Suddenly to dispel this gloom, came brightly a young

Monsieur Dubois, who must have been a persuasive man because they at once gave him *carte blanche* to deal with the matter. In no time, Monsieur Dubois had persuaded Gaby, who was about to appear in a new revue, to wear a costume and headdress confected totally of ostrich feathers.

Her entrance in this plumage on the opening night made such a sensation that an immediate fashion was created, one that flew triumphant through all the capitals of Europe. Dubois, who had signed exclusive contracts with the great couture houses and stores for the supply of feathers, channelled all orders to the South African farm; and he, at least, lived happily ever after.

I last saw Gaby as 'Rosy Rapture' in the name part of the only revue Sir James Barrie ever wrote. She was not wearing the ostrich plumes, now forever her motif, but a small pink feather hat which on her entrance she at once took off and placed over the naked bulb of a table lamp, a 'bit of business' that never failed to send a ripple of pleasure through the audience.

When Nell Gwynne died in 1687 she bequeathed her money to the poor soldiers at Chelsea; in 1923 her sister courtesan, Gaby Delys, left her share of the 'loot' to the poor of Marseilles, her birth-place.

In Lisbon, I had almost given Duncan Orr-Lewis up as lost on the high seas (or, more likely, detained by mermaids) when suddenly he arrived, announcing, even before I opened my mouth, that we were leaving on the *rapide* that evening for Madrid, Barcelona and Marseilles. *Volonté* had already sailed for Southampton. I had been looking forward to the trip because *Volonté* was well found, well crewed and always well provisioned, but I did my best to hide my disappointment. This sudden change of plan was typical of Duncan.

Typically again, Duncan had learned (how and where?) that when the revolution was over many of the embalmed bodies of the former Portuguese royal family had been dumped in the crypt of a small and ancient church outside the city. Eventually we found the place, the Church of S. Vincente. After driving into the hills and a rapid exchange of a large wad of escudos from Duncan's wallet to the folds of the sacristan's cassock, we were led down a narrow, musty staircase to the crypt.

As our eyes became used to the light of three guttering candles, we saw we were amid a clutter of black wooden boxes, each with

The Kirchner Girl

Ruby and the contraband

Gaby Deslys—the girl who rocked a young king's throne

Godfrey, Sir Ronald Grayson, Ambrose and Father Woodlock, S.J.

a glass lid. They were lying at random, scattered in dusty disarray as if carelessly discarded by a sodality of drunken undertakers.

Duncan suddenly whispered, for it was a place of whispers and ourselves were in a sense entombed. 'Take a look at this one.' He was bending over one of the coffins, tilting it for a better view. As I lowered my candle the wax spluttered over the glass, so it was through a waxen lacework that I saw the stuffed corpse of Dom Carlos, Manuel's uncle, still with tarnished decorations and medals pinned to a faded uniform; from a puffed face his eyes protruded, gazing up at me with glazed surprise.

I had never seen Dom Carlos alive, but it was not surprising, after his trunk-cavities and tissue-cells, his groin, arms and base of neck had been filled with several gallons of embalming solution by vascular injection with a six-inch hollow needle, that his overall expression should be one of startled discontent.

Duncan had, as it were, tasted blood and he was now pulling and pushing the coffins briskly in search of more. I sensed rather than smelt, in a wave of nausea, the aromatic stench of oriental spices and long-forgotten drugs: enemies (unlike Baudelaire's worms) of putrefaction. It was beautiful afterwards to step into the lemon-coloured air with the city spread below; the houses seeming to tumble grey, blue, white, pink, down to the distant banks of the Tagus, itself a moving band of green, glittering in the sunshine. In a burst of elation, I embraced the old sacristan who had unconsciously guided us through the corridors of death into the reality and glory of life.

Back at the hotel, Duncan was rather amused when an American came up to me in the bar and enquired, 'Did you ever live in Paris?' and I replied, 'I think so.' 'Damn it, man,' the American said, 'you must know.' To which I then enquired: 'Is that the place with the Mona Lisa and a big tower like Blackpool?' to which he, in turn, hissed: 'I've never been to Blackpool but I had the apartment below yours in the Rue des Eaux and I've been trying to catch up on my sleep ever since, you bastard.'

I have always enjoyed the unexpected reply. When a fellow Harrovian was leaving the school the headmaster asked him what he intended doing.

'I'm going up to Cambridge, sir, where I'll be reading for the bar.'

'Splendid,' the headmaster replied, 'it's so much better than going with loose women.'

But it is the mild-mannered man who can deliver the most stinging rebuke. Laurie Lee, the poet and author of *Cider with Rosie*, when told that a reviewer called Kingsley Amis had published a vicious attack on a book he had written about Spain, looked puzzled for a moment and then mused: 'Kingsley Amis. It sounds like a very small railway station.'

We caught the *rapide* with a few minutes to spare, Duncan's invariable manner of travel. That night the train raced forward on the unyielding track with booming vibration, crashing over junctions and echoing the last hollow notes of a tunnel as the grinding bogies rattled and swung over steel-laced bridgeways. As I lay in my berth in the green dimness, I could not rid myself of the cadaverous memory of the crypt. It was almost as if I were still inhaling the stench escaping from the coffins, lavender, oil, Venetian turpentine, and camomile mixed with the faint sigh of visceral gases. The Egyptians, masters of embalming, had striven pyramidally to ensure the privacy of the tomb; what we had seen was a monstrous insult to the dignity of Man in death.

I had already inspected Lenin in his Muscovite tomb, after queueing for three hours in a driving wind traversing Red Square. In his glass casket he lay serene and commonplace; but he'd have surely looked less placid had he known that Stalin (that yellow-eyed monster) was to ease himself into the vacant throne as chairman and managing director of the largest butchery business in the history of inhumanity; until Hitler Incorporated started in expert opposition a decade later.

If one believes in the sanctity of air, earth, fire and water, the only burial rite that pays homage to all and contaminates none is that of the Parsees. On the Tower of Silence outside Bombay, the bodies of the dead are exposed to the vultures, God's creatures and mankind's beneficent scavengers. Within the hour bones are stripped bare, and these the sun scorches to fragility and the wind disperses the dust. Though vultures are not birds I would keep as pets, when I die I would prefer to be picked clean in the sunshine by one of these, than to be devoured by worms, *anciens amis de la pourriture*, in the great darkness of the grave.

Often in Spain I would watch the vultures staggering around

the white carcass of a donkey, too replete to take wing, while the boys of San Roque from a safe distance stoned them to death.

We picked up Duncan's Bentley in Marseilles next day, and as we left the environs of this great southern city, I recalled the international occasion when I had heard *La Bohème* sung there in three languages at the Opera House; Rodolfo in Italian, Marcel in German and Mimi in English; describing her simple life she uses the charming phrase 'I have a little chamber'. This would have surely delighted Puccini.

We dined that night in Paris with Niki Katkoff. Niki's mother was Lady Egerton, who had married a former British Minister in St Petersburg and now ran a famous *maison de couture* in the Rue Royale known as Paul Caret. When Niki had been naval attaché at the Russian Embassy in Chesham Place in London, he had taught me to drink large quantities of vodka from very small cut-glass bottles with the double eagle and the Imperial crown on the label; these bottles, apart from their content, would have looked well on any woman's dressing-table. He had married a beautiful Russian who sang with such charm it was said that the nightingales would stop in mid-song to listen; but the most impressive moment I spent with him was at the Crillon when he introduced me to Diaghilev and even addressed the great impresario as 'Sergei'.

That night, having driven 800 kilometres, we arrived at the Hermitage at Le Touquet; but not to sleep; we were both too tired for that.

Le Touquet had always charmed the English but it never captivated the French. In about 1910, a delightful English family called Stoneham began developing the whole of the forest area of Le Touquet, building villas and hotels, interfering little with the beauty of the forest nor encroaching on the small seaside resort of Paris-Plage. A fairly natural links was laid out with a clubhouse and hotel. A casino followed, great hotels arose among the trees (the Hermitage, the Westminster and the Picardy), the wealthy English came for the golf by day and the gambling by night. Buck's Club ran a special long weekend for their members, quartered at the Golf Hotel.

The Prince of Wales was staying at the Westminster. He was always about wherever the lights were brightest, the women the loveliest and the golf the greenest. He had inherited not from his father but from his grandfather a zest for living and an insatiable curiosity about the life led by those who would not normally come within his circle.

Luigi, one of the great restaurateurs, used to reserve a table nightly for him at the Embassy Club in Bond Street, a dinner-dance club unsurpassed in Europe for the excellence of its food, wine and cigars. Once in the early hours of one morning his table had been given to a party of attractive Americans; there was consternation when the Prince of Wales and his brother George turned up; but H.R.H. immediately waived his *droit de seigneur* and convivially joined the party.

Though he often appeared shy and nervous he had a graciousness about him which, with his good looks, charmed everyone. To the consternation of his father's intimates and courtiers this young man had friends amongst theatricals, bookies, acrobats, jockeys, in fact anyone who was likely to interest him; for his public duties (and a life rarely concealed from the public eye) could only be borne if moments of complete relaxation could be snatched from officialdom.

The war had brought him into closer contact with the so-called common man than any previous prince or sovereign, and his sympathetic attitude to the workers and the miners in South Wales angered the politicians; although it was only unorthodox they preferred to look on it as unconstitutional. But he had fought alongside his own countrymen in my own division and he understood them better than the politicians did. On a visit to a stricken industrial district a trades union leader suggested it might be unwise of him to wear his fur-lined greatcoat. 'I don't want to be told what to wear,' he replied. 'I know you mean well but I know better than you what they want to see me wearing.'

Like all people who have good friends he had enemies, and when his father George V was told that his son and heir to the throne had played the drums one night at the Kit Cat Club it was rumoured that the interview which followed would have shaken even the King's valet, who for years had taken the full impact of the monarch's quarterdeck language.

In America the King and Queen were known as George and the Dragon; possibly because of Queen Mary's taste in hats, she was looked on as humourless and unbending. In fact of the two she was by far the more gracious and had a lively sense of humour. The King was strictly conventional; his goodwill and sailor's bonhomie were confined to close friends and naval associates. I happened to be in a Bath antique shop when Queen Mary and Lady Airlie came in. The owner hurriedly left me to receive her but when she asked him whether he had anything interesting to show her, the shock of this unexpected visit was too much for him and he stood gazing at her, made speechless by visions of 'By Royal Appointment' until she came to his rescue by saying, 'At this rate we're not going to get anywhere.' She was a great collector of antiques, particularly those she coveted in her friends' houses and which she invariably carried away with her; it was rumoured in the trade that those who enjoyed 'By Royal Appointment' were careful to hide anything liable to take her fancy, because of her tendency to look on purchases as gifts.

The 'Pragger-Wagger', as the prince was known as an undergraduate at Oxford, was acclaimed by the masses of all countries wherever he went. He was what might now be described as 'pop royalty', the precursor of Jack Kennedy; he had the same charisma, the spirit of youth in whom his own generation had found a leader. Speaking of Lord Lascelles, his brother-in-law who married Princess Mary, he said, 'Every day Lascelles gets royaler and royaler, and every day I get commoner and commoner.'

Like all his family he could be remarkably caustic when it suited him. I was lunching one day with Buckmaster (who founded Buck's Club) when he came into the dining-room with his aide-de-camp, General Trotter. Buck had been mulling over the idea of starting a Buck's golf course in the Thames Valley. 'Ask H.R.H. what he thinks about the idea,' Buck whispered to Trotter as they moved to their table. After luncheon, standing in my stall in the men's room, I heard H.R.H.'s voice behind me: 'Your club's a good idea, Buck, but I advise you not to hang your hat up on me.'

He detested his royalty being used as an exploitation gimmick; although it was his own revolution in men's dress that has ended (like all revolutions) in an anti-climax, and the slovenliness and scruffiness of the youth of our day. He took, as it were, the starch out of fashion, made the informal formal and added colour to the clothes-rack; soft collars with dinner jackets, bold bright checks, startling jumpers and hugely knotted ties, still known as 'the

Windsor'. He, too, like all the English, loved Le Touquet and its forest; but to tell the truth, it could never compete with Deauville, having neither a yacht harbour, a race-course nor an opera house, without which no French resort could be considered elegant.

Louis Drexel once took a villa in Le Touquet, but the weekend flood of hearty wealthy English, flowing in on Fridays and ebbing out 'hung-over' on Sunday evenings, was in hectic contrast to the smooth seasonal patterns of Deauville and La Boule and the autumn dignities of Biarritz.

That morning after my arrival it was delightful for me to stroll into the Le Touquet Casino into which, in 1916, I had been carried on a stretcher, a casualty from the Salient. It was then a hospital, presided over by the Duchess of Westminster. Almost at once I ran into Billie Neilson, a Liverpool friend. Apart from his business activities he had backed those enormously successful Aldwych farces, *Tons of Money*, *Thark* and the rest. These farces had an enormous vogue with the superb partnership of Tom Walls and Ralph Lynn, 'supported' (as the theatrical papers say) by Mary Brough. Tom Walls won the Derby when April the Fifth romped home at 30–1 in the year 1931.

My friend Clifford Bagot Gray and I had written a play which opened (on a trial run) in Cambridge. We were unhappy about it because it had been written with the Aldwych company in view; we had as principals Jack Hobbs and Mercia Swinburn, both magnificent comedy players but with no experience of farce. We commissioned Ralph Lynn to put a bit of pep into the play and he agreed, charging 200 guineas for two days' rehearsing, plus his expenses in Cambridge. The play, when it eventually opened and shut at the Duke of York's Theatre, was a magnificent failure, best forgotten; and to console Clifford and me, I suppose. Ralph Lynn, no spendthrift, nearly bought us a drink in the bar.

After champagne that early morning in Le Touquet, Neilson put £500 in plaques into my hands and asked me to play for the party. At the chemin de fer table my luck was completely out. The cards were running against me and I managed only too successfully to lose the £500 in the hour. I thought then of the time in Monte Carlo when I met a man who had just broken the bank, as they say, at one of the roulette tables. Breaking the bank at the Casino meant that play at the table stopped until the bank was replenished. The whole process was performed slowly and with the maximum publicity so that the news could quickly spread. To every punter it was the moment to try out his lucky system; for every gambler is at heart superstitious whether he plays to a system or not.

I happened to be with Guido, who ran the Royalty Bar in Monte Carlo, when this lucky man came in and I was introduced to him. I remember my first impression was of a dim, rather ordinary little fellow, clearly unaccustomed to his surroundings; he appeared slightly out of focus, like a figure superimposed by some photographic trick on an alien background. He appeared to be too elusive for the part he had been called upon to play, because breaking the bank at Monte Carlo thrusts a man into instant, if temporary, prominence. Overnight he becomes an object of interest and is automatically drawn into the orbit of the journalist, the press photographer, the *restaurateur*, the hanger-on, the brothel-keeper, the *demi-mondaine* and the crook. I could see he was both suffering and enjoying, basking and cringing in the merciless floodlight of his notoriety.

Arthur (for such was his name) had a story to tell. 'I went into the Casino,' he explained, 'to play my system—twenty-five francs goes on the *transversales* on the low numbers and I insure on *passe* for the same amount. If the high numbers are coming up I go for them and insure myself on *manque*. That way I have only three numbers against me and zero; but if one of those four turn up I've lost the lot.' We drank our martinis while they were still cold and I ordered more.

'I played for an hour and I was up twenty-five francs, when I was seized with an irresistible impulse to back number 17. The trouble with a system is that it gets too boring.' He paused thoughtfully. 'You know it was no surprise to me when 17 turned up.'

It was then the complications started piling up, because the croupier wanted to know what he wanted done with his winnings. Arthur wanted two plaques left *en plein* on the number 2, so he cried across the table, 'Two, two!'

'I've never been much good at the lingo,' he confessed, 'it sounds all wrong to me but I know that "two" in English is "all" in French; so when I saw him flicking and pushing all my winnings back on to 17 I shouted, "Enough, enough!" and the bloody fool thought I was saying "Neuf, neuf", and shoved them all on to 9.'

He took a gulp at his martini and rocked his head slowly from side to side, chuckling. 'When the wheel stopped spinning and the croupier shouted, "*Numéro neuf, rouge, impair et manque*", you could have knocked me down with a sledge-hammer.' With his original twenty-five francs he had won 60,000. 'You'd never believe it, the way people swarmed round me slapping my back and touching me with *jetons* to bring them luck.'

Our martinis and the story of his good fortune inspired me to invite him to luncheon, so I took him to Ciro's where he was warmly welcomed. Here he told me the unremarkable story of his life, one only interrupted in its course as that of a civil servant by annual holidays and timely periods of ill-health.

On the evening of the following day I found him sitting disconsolately outside the Café de Paris. He had lost every sou. The Casino authorities had promised him a *viatique* (a travel voucher) only after he had been taken to each table at which he had lost, where each croupier had to verify his losses before he could be given a third-class ticket back to London, together with a packet of rather stale sandwiches left over from the Casino bar.

By this time I looked on Arthur as a friend who must be spared this humiliating experience; when I told him I would pay his hotel bill and advance money for his journey, he was very relieved. Indeed, to celebrate, we ordered a bottle of champagne and a little later I left him at his hotel to settle his bill. As it was still fairly early I thought I'd try my luck in the public rooms, known as the 'kitchen'. Here in the smokeless atmosphere, the air, heavy and inert, was charged with the disagreeable exudations of tense, excited bodies, and the stench of clothes moist with sweat (as difficult to describe accurately as a deadly, tasteless drug), so I moved to the Sporting Club.

As I had said farewell to Arthur at his hotel, and left him, comparatively sober, packing his bags, I was surprised and embarrassed when I noticed him seated at one of the tables. I sought to hide, but he had already seen me and soon we were sharing yet another bottle, for it transpired that he had, in the meantime, won back all his losses, and was well in credit. We were soon most happily *in vino*. Discretion gone, I rendered to the American bar at large that speech from Julius Caesar, known to every schoolboy, croupier, absconding financier, archduke and *poule-de-luxe,* which I thought appropriate to the occasion: 'There is a tide in the affairs of men which taken at the flood. . . .' The applause that followed was no less appreciated by me because it came solely from my friend Arthur. The last I saw of him was in the cold grey dawn, swallowed in the darkness of a *bôite de nuit.*

At Le Touquet that morning I learned yet another thing when I lost Billie Neilson's £500: never play with another man's money unless you've won it from him in the first place.

Next day, having seen Duncan off on the Boulogne ferry, on impulse I caught the train to Paris and then the night train to Rome. My father had been there during the War as Director of Ship Repairs, at the time I had carried my first bag as a temporary King's Messenger to the Embassy at Porta Pia; and I was reminded, too, of that member of his staff who could scrawl *graffiti* in twenty different languages; and like Henry Miller's fantastic friend was unable to remember in what language he had first read *Alice in Wonderland.*

But now it wasn't the Grand Hotel, the Excelsior, the Borghese Gardens or St John Lateran that was drawing me back to Rome. It was the little square into which I had wandered one day earlier that summer. It had been sleeping under a broiling noonday sun, a haze of heat quivering over the motionless dust that penetrated every crack and crevice of the baked stones; no eddy disturbed the drowsy air. Then unexpectedly I had walked into a pool of blue shadow under a sweetly resinous cypress; here there was a little flower-booth and beside it, stretched on a rush mat, a girl lay fast asleep. In that secret moment while I looked down at her sleeping eyes I felt like an intruder; yet quite unconsciously, in the act of sleep itself, she had created a masterpiece. Without waking her I slipped a note sufficient to pay for all her flowers into a small, brown hand.

As the Rome express carried me south I liked to think I was hurrying back to a windless altar where I had left a candle burning; in truth I just wanted to see the girl with her eyes open and her lips smiling in the same magical shadow cast by the straw hat she had been wearing as she lay asleep.

The next day I walked into the square. A sharp wind was blowing and the first autumn rains were pelting on to the glistening stones. The flower-stall was no longer there, but when I sheltered under the cypress the smell of resin was even more pungent in the rain. In my foolish dreams and in my youthful conceit I must have believed the universe was created for myself alone and that time would stand still at my convenience. I was learning that things that don't happen can be as important in your life as those that do.

CHAPTER VII

Falling in love again . . .

NOËL COWARD

Despite all these frivolities and excursions with no alarms I was now well into my second book and suffering the usual agonies and ecstasies, but I was happy to be back at the villa Pins Blancs with the Drexel family.

I bought myself an Amilcar which, like most French cars of that period, would submit to every kind of cruelty and neglect: all I needed was a car that would start and stop, climb and descend the cultivated terraced foothills of the littoral and the steep mountains of the hinterland.

Every day I set off, my luncheon basket stocked with pâté, cheese, fresh rolls, fruit and wine, pens and paper. My expeditions would take me through the beautiful little villages of Provence and the Saracen towns of the Alpes Maritimes. Usually I avoided the coastal resorts, driving to Grasse lying sleepily in the sun on its ledge of the foothills, and on to the entrancing blue shadow that marked the Gorge de Loup.

Here H. G. Wells had built a villa, Loubidou, for his charming, talented and volatile friend, Odette Keun, who once confounded that horrible man Joynson Hicks. Jix, as he was unaffectionately called, was the Home Secretary of the period and engaged in mortal conflict with contemporary art and artists and their *moeurs*. D. H. Lawrence's paintings were seized by the police and the gallery owner prosecuted; a harmless poet and pretender to the Hungarian throne, Count Potocki de Montakk, who affected long hair and regal habiliments, was flung into jail for publishing some mild erotica. Jix, together with his ally, James Douglas, book reviewer of the *Sunday Express*, stern moralists both with complementarily filthy minds, were determined to 'clean up' Britain. Their particular target was Radclyffe Hall's *The Well of Loneliness*, a charming and sad story of two women in love with each other. Douglas said that he would sooner give arsenic to a child of his than let it read the book; and Jix launched a prosecution.

Odette met this ghastly man at a dinner party and listened to him declaring that he was determined to stamp out this 'filthy lesbianism'. 'But Jix,' said Odette, 'it ees not filthy, it ees very clean, what zey do ees this . . .' and launched into a clinical account of the lesbian act that should have broadened his mind, even if it put him off his dinner.

I was drawn up the steep winding road to Gourdon like steel to a magnet, for it was these sinister heights I had used as a background for my novel *Scarlet Livery*.

I knew every metre of the road through Antibes to Nice, often turning off to have an aperitif at Vence. It was here later that D. H. Lawrence was buried. My friend, Frank Budgen, painter and author of that wonderful autobiography, *Myselves when Young*, was in the neighbourhood at the time and, hearing that an English writer whom he did not know was about to be buried, went to the funeral out of solidarity. He said it was the most depressing event: a box dropped in a hole and earth shovelled over it; with not even a newspaperman to report the end of a genius.

I became a familiar figure in the Condamine in Monaco where I drank in the cafés after I had lit my candles in the little church of S. Devoté, which stands in the shadows of the Ravin de Garmettes under the railway bridge linking Monaco with Monte Carlo. Here a small stream tumbles merrily down from the upper ledges where the sun strikes, and wild flowers star the saffron rocks and butterflies paint the air.

There were writers of all sorts along the coast. W. J. Locke lived at Les Acades on the Californie. He wrote many best-sellers of the day including *The Beloved Vagabond*, which Sir Herbert

Tree adapted for the stage and played the name part at His Majesty's. Baroness Orczy lived in Monte Carlo with her husband and her son, who was at Harrow with me. I suggested she should write a story about the descendant of her great character, Sir Percy Blakeney, the Scarlet Pimpernel, who should be rescuing people out of Russia. She was not interested; for her history ended at the French Revolution with the dull thud of the guillotine. Phillips Oppenheim, the Ian Fleming of his day, also lived in Monte Carlo, and on the Menton road Biasco Ibanez, the author of *The Four Horsemen of the Apocalypse*, had built himself a grandiose villa. Rudolph Valentino was round and about, the ex-waiter film star, who played lead in the picture and after Ibanez' death became a cult-idol for the frustrated middle-aged matrons of the world's middle classes. Ronald Colman, another object of female adoration, was excellent company and often used to stay at the Carlton in Cannes. He was so short in stature that all his leading ladies had to be near-midgets.

My brother Denys had taken the St James's Theatre for a season with Lyn Harding, a famous Shakespearean actor, who also had a continuous success as Doctor Rylott in the frequent revivals of *The Speckled Band*. They were casting a play by Haddon Chambers, a well-known playwright of that time. One of the actors auditioned for the juvenile lead (at £20 a week) was Ronald Colman. They considered him too small for the part; in an effort to reverse the decision he pleaded desperately that he had a full range of evening dress. A year later Denys, because of the instant success he'd made in Hollywood, couldn't have engaged him for £20,000 a week.

Michael Arlen, author of that international best-seller, *The Green Hat,* was often in Cannes. He said to me one day apropos of his recent marriage: 'I'd kicked around with other fellows' wives for so long I decided I'd like to have one of my own.' Questioned by a passport official in New York about his profession, he replied: 'I'm one of the Armenian atrocities.'

Sometimes my wanderings took me to the little town of Castillon; or to Sospel, where I would stroll through the narrow lanes between tall houses, where the people went about their business in everlasting twilight.

I was always alone on my expeditions. To have an agreeable companion can add to enjoyment, but to be alone adds to perception; one learns to examine everything with Proustian eyes, sharpening into focus every minute detail, every reflection of light moving on shade and shade moving on light until even the colour of the air is registered in the retina; as with a painter, mind and eye co-ordinate instinctively. If I was not always the patient observer I strove to be, unconsciously I was preparing myself for a life of aloneness in the future.

People over their wine will sometimes clink glasses because it is a human instinct to add sound where there is already taste and smell. Thus I sometimes found it comforting to talk aloud to myself; but it could also be interesting in a café to listen to the comments of those around when I wrote my order down and handed it to the waiter in the manner of a man deaf and dumb. In the discussion that usually followed I would often hear it said that it would be preferable to be blind than without speech or hearing. Certainly our beloved Uncle Tom Harrington, who had been blind from an early age, always told us he'd rather be blind than deaf. If any of these afflictions overtook me I would infinitely prefer deafness. Most knowledge worth remembering can be gained through books, and through sight all sounds can be recalled, the music of a brook, the cry of wood pigeons, the opening bars of Beethoven's Fifth, the sound of children playing in the meadow.

For me the real tragedy would be to lose the sense of smell; my memories would be dead were I never to experience the recurrence of those first and never-to-be-forgotten smells of childhood, fresh rolls and coffee on the morning air, hayfields at harvest time, the tang of manure, new milk and sweating horses, the sickly, stuffy smell of the village shop, the innocent perfume of Mother's gloves, the aroma of Havana tobacco seeping up to our bedrooms after dinner, the fragrance of the first of the mimosa, the cottony atmosphere and the unexpected whiff of machine oil in the sewing-room, the pungency of the morning papers in the hall, piles of fresh lavender-scented linen, the spicy scents in the kitchen with the Sunday sirloin twisting and roasting on the spit, and the linoleum smell of the servants' hall. These and the countless other smells that come with manhood to remind me of joys and sorrows, and moments of peaceful longing when the aromatic smell of incense rises to the heavens in the dark cathedral; and the scent of the curly head beside me on the pillow creeps into my dreams. Nor would I want to forget the evil smells that sting the mind alive with memories, the stench of rancid mutton fat in a Caribbean port, a bug-ridden bed in Mexico, dirty clothes on dirty bodies in the Moscow Metro on a wet day, or the stench of a vulture's entrails bubbling in a tropical sun. Taste, sight, sound and smell, are all part of living, and the truth is we need every animal sense; when misfortune strikes we must be armed to the teeth, the eyes, the ears and the nostrils. It has always seemed strange to me that Degas with his genius should have disliked smells of every description : even the sleepy garden perfumes of a summer's evening.

My solitude (to which I believed myself resigned) was not to last for long; for in the natural course of events she appeared one afternoon out of the twilight streets of Sospel into the sunshine on the edge of the town. She was walking between a row of green poplars and the blue shadows cast on the long white wall opposite where I had parked my car. It was as if I had entered some magnetic field; her vibrations aroused in me an immediate and exquisite response, and when I spoke it seemed I had been waiting for her and she had expected me to be there.

Her name was Mariette and she had only recently moved to the town with her parents. She worked at home as an *embroideuse* (shades of Mimi and Rodolfo) employed by an *haute couturière* in Menton. She seldom visited the garish coast and knew about the way of life led by the international set only from what she read in the *Eclairer de Nice*. Every now and then the inherent shrewdness of the Provençal peasant broke through her natural delicacy and reserve; at the first opportunity she would discard her shoes and walk barefoot. It was beautiful to watch her walk : she put the weight first on her heels instead of on her toes, so that there was a superb balance and dignity about her progress. She walked like a woman with fire in her belly and prepared to kick the ground from under her feet. As our friendship grew her constant anxiety was, naturally, the money I was spending, the only cause of friction between us. Several times she took me to meet her parents and I was conscious of a slight strain in the atmosphere. They were, I realized, anxious about her future. Once when alone her mother said to me, 'I hope you are a good man.' I quickly examined my conscience, but all I could reply was : 'I try to be a kind man.' I ceased visiting them because their sense of unease seemed to grow in proportion to the gifts I gave; but they never forbade her to meet me. I showed her an aspect of life wholly new to her and it gave me the illusion that I, too, was seeing through her eyes. Each day her awakening to new sights, sounds and smells was like the miraculous opening of a desert flower.

There were days when we drove to the coast or into the mountains; but more often we stayed in the foothills with our luncheon basket. Sometimes at the end of the day she would sing Provençal love songs in a low, husky voice with her brown eyes heavy with longing and I would watch the movement of her lips; for her mouth, even in shadow, was clearly defined, and when she had finished her song on the last note, her lips would remain sleepily parted in the shape of a lover's kiss.

Then one day we came to the Café de la Terrasse for the second time. The *patronne* was one of those women (France's gift to civilization, agreeable and understanding and alive with tender memories) who appear like the good fairy in the lives of young lovers when they are most in need of her. Without being asked she immediately led us to an upstairs room. Dusting the little oval mirror over the fireplace and turning back the counterpane on the bed she suggested we might wish to rest after our long drive. Thereafter there were always flowers in the room, the counterpane turned back and the little oval mirror polished. From then on it became our home, where we lived a secret life within our own.

She took to bringing her embroidery with her and I was persuaded it was to please me that she worked in colours which set off her dark beauty; she was no peaches-and-cream girl from England or America, but an earthy peasant with the sun and wine and the passionate south in her blood. In her company the days passed remarkably gently, for she had her embroidery (there is nothing so restful as a woman sewing in silence) and I had my pens and paper. Our relationship was complete and during the short, sweet time we were together it was as if we were living within a spell.

One morning to please me, because she knew she had been a little bitchy the previous day, we lunched at the Carlton in Cannes. Her clothes were charmingly unconventional for that dressy place, and I was conscious of the men's admiring stares

Tristram before inspecting the Downside OTC—'the finest London Provost Marshal ever'

'It's such a lovely day! Let's go out and kill something!'

'In a flash of cellophane the roses vanished down a smoke stack'

and the women's cool appraisal, as their eyes undressed her from the scarlet ribbon in her hair to her sun-bronzed feet as she walked barefoot into the restaurant.

She appeared to be quite unconscious of the sensation she had created, but when she was seated at the table she leaned back with a mischievous expression of triumph, which clearly said, 'Didn't I do that beautifully?'; and, as I watched her, I realized here was that most delightful thing, a girl 'sitting pretty'. Confronted with the array of different knives, forks and spoons, she gave me secret enquiring glances, looking so beautiful that the waiter hovered about the table taking so long to serve us that I had to ask him whether he'd had one too many.

She ate everything with the appetite of a hungry child, particularly the *baiser de vierge*, vanilla cream meringue under a brittle veil of spun sugar, perfumed with crystallized rose leaves and white violets. Throughout the meal she had been completely self-possessed as I would expect her to be; but when we were back in the car she pressed close to me as if she had submitted to an ordeal that she would not willingly undergo again.

The days passed, my book progressed and her work continued. Then one evening something happened of so peculiar a nature that I can only describe it as inexplicable.

I had called for her as usual in the morning and with our luncheon basket we had set off in the direction of a former childhood home she wished me to see. On the way there I saw the ideal place to rest and lunch: a hillside, well wooded, with sufficient water in a stream for our needs and in the distant line of blue the middle-sea. I suggested we stayed here awhile, but she objected almost hysterically. I usually let her have her way; but, knowing that unless someone makes up their mind where to picnic one can be driving round all day, I was adamant. In some ways I regretted my decision because she hardly spoke during the whole day and showed the fretfulness of a spoiled child. Towards evening, the fire of smouldering discontent between us burst into flame and a quarrel followed over something trivial; so in anger I left her to pack the baskets.

Nearby there was a small wood looking particularly beautiful because it was silhouetted against a windy sunset. I walked towards it, and as I did so I heard her cry begging me to come back. There was an anguish in her voice I had not heard before, but paying no heed to her cries I went on into the wood through a natural leafy passage. Inside there was a silence which was uncanny; I realized there were no birds in the trees nor creatures in the undergrowth. Sleepily I was aware of her cries, now louder and even more hysterical; and I could see her grey shadow at the entrance to the woodland tunnel. When I turned to follow on my path I was facing what looked like a broken swing; one rope held the wooden seat just clear of the ground and the other hung loose, its end frayed, from the branch of a tree. I touched it, but it crumbled into dust through my fingers. I stood motionless in the unnatural silence. Then I heard a strange sound, subterranean and oozing, like water imprisoned and seeking to escape. Already I felt myself squelching in the undergrowth and sinking in swamp. Instinctively I tried to lift my feet from the roots entangling them. Then the clearing in which I stood beside the swing seemed slowly to expand into a circular space, and as the trees retreated into a surrounding girdle I was aware of a cold, glassy surface forming over the undergrowth, imprisoning me in an embrace, warm and salty as the sea; and I felt my body in suspended consciousness surrender itself slowly on to its bosom in the gathering twilight. The wooden seat of the swing was afloat.

In this nightmare I would have grasped this object to break my dream, but when I tried to do so it nudged me like a gipsy begging; swept by, turning slowly in lazy eddies; and I was alone. It was then I noticed the second rope, the frayed and hanging one that had first given me a sense of danger. Moving towards me it was slowly coiling its limbless way on the glassy surface. I was not past caring but dreaded any snake or creature that moved like one; I was drowning in a nightmare out of which I couldn't swim my way, nor could I stop its round and scaly surface slowly encircling my neck in a running noose that tightened into a hangman's knot, and I knew death had me by the throat. At the same moment I heard my name said, first in a whisper like a shiver of leaves through the trees, then growing louder, until suddenly I knew she was beside me, leading me with trembling hands down the tunnel and out of the wood. I felt her brushing the leaves off my clothes. 'You should never have gone into the wood,' she kept repeating; 'this is a bad place. You should never have gone into the wood.' She took me to the car.

Now I could see her clearly and everything about us came

into everyday focus. I helped her stow away the baskets and slowly we drove home through the blue Provençal dusk to the Café de la Terrasse. She ordered a bottle of wine to comfort me, but it was not on the terrace she told me the story of the wood, but in our room seated beneath the little oval mirror, kneeling beside me. I could see she had no wish to speak of it, but she had no choice : I must be told. In the wood two young lovers, a fisherman and his girl, used to meet. Then one day the boy was lost at sea and the girl hanged herself with the swing rope at their trysting place. She herself had heard the story of the wood as a little girl, for it was known and believed throughout the district that the place was haunted, and none would enter it—and yet she had braved it in search of me.

When I heard the story, all the more moving because it was told in one breathless sentence, I felt a frigid breath passing through my hair. We never spoke of it again nor did we drive again on that road.

There followed days and nights of languid enchantment but at first bluntly, then sharply like pointed teeth, I felt the wolf of restlessness gnawing into me and the great longing to be on my way, warming my body with excitement and chilling my heart with remorse. How was she to know, much less understand the roving spirit that even in those far-off days consumed me and was one day to destroy me.

Sometimes we would sit over our wine in silence in the calm loneliness of each other's company, under the cool, patched, faded awning, each dreaming a different dream until the little village street was blurred in smoky shadows. One evening we had gone to our room and as we looked out, standing side by side, on the deserted road, I gently touched her lips with my mouth as I had so often done to awaken her from sleep. She turned and looked into the little oval mirror; and—why, I do not know—I had the strange feeling that this might be the last time we were to look into its depths together. Mirrored so, she gazed at me without surprise or sorrow. Unlike myself, she knew for certain it was the end.

CHAPTER VIII

A foutra for the world, and worldlings base!
I speak of Africa and golden joys.

SHAKESPEARE

That night, back at the Drexels, there was a letter from Father inviting me to London: an invitation from Father was a royal command. He probably imagined I was idling my time away in bars, cafés, *cantinas*, *ratskelleren*, blind-tigers, cabarets, bordellos and other places of amusement when in fact I was devoting half my time to a lovely bare-foot peasant girl and the other half to writing a book. And as everyone knows, a man in love has little time to spare visiting pothouses, saloons, wine shops, night clubs, blind-pigs, *bistros* and brothels.

I tried to talk with Mariette, but she had seen something in the little oval mirror that I had not seen—the conflict between our love and my compulsive wanderlust. She made no effort to hold me and only smiled a little sadly when I swore I'd be back within days. I watched her go. She had told me she would write to me that very night to my London hotel.

Was Father throwing me a lifeline? In spite of his good looks and wealth he was essentially a lonely man. He wanted me in London and I must not, as I had done so often in the past, disappoint him.

Once, years before, we had met in Ostend by chance, booked in at the same hotel. He had been delighted I was there because he had been persuaded by one of his many Belgian friends (he was a Commander of the Order of Leopold) to buy an enormous car. This mammoth vehicle must have been the grandsire of the prolific and loathsome international family of dormobiles that now assist the total pollution of the countryside and beaches of England, Europe and America. He suggested we should try out the mechanical monster on a drive to Brussels. I felt his disappointment when I excused myself; for no better reason than upstairs in my bedroom, my check coat was hanging in a cupboard with my bowler hat, my lemon-coloured gloves lay with my racing-glasses, and because that morning, walking on the Digue, I had met a dusky little wanton (with rosy lips, velvet eyes and colouring that betrayed delightfully her Congolese ancestry) whom I had promised to take to the races.

This was only a minor disappointment among the many I had caused him, for which only the unthinking cruelty of youth could be offered as excuse.

Most things happen to me outside by volition. I lived, it seemed, in a dreaming pattern of sounds and smells over which I had no control. Was this to be the end of my life in France after months of playing and working with people I loved? Was this the end of my love affair whose life had been brief as a flower? Autumn had come; along the coast the hotel shutters were going up, the summer casinos closing, the leaves of the plane trees falling; and somewhere in my heart I knew that a lovely chapter in my life had closed.

I packed my bags and my manuscript, booked by ticket on the Blue Train, and said my sad farewells to Nancy and Louis, Eugène, Jeanne and Marie and the Elysian gardener.

A few days later I was at the Cavendish Hotel in London reading a letter from Mariette. She told me a marriage had been arranged for her; he was a good man, she wrote, a prosperous wine merchant living in Castillon, and she hoped she would make him a good wife, bear him children and be happy.

As I held her letter in my hand I felt the future confronting me like an enemy. Slowly I was realizing with a great bitterness that love has its statute of limitations; and in making one thing you are often destroying another—like the reed that gives forth its music only after it has been hacked out of the river. Somewhere I had read:

Aber wenn du sagst
Ich liebe dich:
So müss ich weinen
*Bitterlich!**

In the frowsy anonymity of my sitting-room at the Cavendish I poured myself a whisky from the sideboard and drank it; then seeing the vast oblong Victorian mirror (so different to the little oval one in France) I hurled my empty glass at the unhappy man reflected in it.

For a moment there was nothing but the sound of shattering glass; then gradually, like the opening of a flower in a slow-motion picture, there appeared a silver design in the shape of a glittering cross. I went to bed uncomforted and slept like a dog.

Father's reasons for recalling me to London were twofold: he was in the process of buying the publishing firm of Eveleigh Nash, in which my brother Brian was working; and, when negotiations were completed, desired me to take an active interest in it. Until then he was to indulge (vicariously) his love of travel.

Father had become engrossed in the life of Cecil Rhodes; he had read all known works on this ambitious and ruthless Englishman, and for no better reason he had decided that my young twin brothers, Ambrose and Godfrey (accompanied by me) should follow in the footsteps of this great empire-builder from Oxford (that city in defence of whose marmalade I had fought in the First World War) to his lonely grave in the Matopo Hills.

It is only fair to say, however, that though he had an incorrigible habit of interfering in our lives, brothers and sisters alike, it was usually in the form of some fresh foreign delight he had conceived for our edification; because he believed it was only through travel that our eyes could be opened to the wonders of the world, and our minds moulded to accept concepts alien to our hereditary beliefs.

I soon found the invitation was a mere courtesy: he had already booked us a suite on the *Ubena*, a German ship. This was most surprising. Was it not well known that in a crisis all foreign crews invariably panicked and took to the boats before

* But when you say 'I love you', then I must weep, bitterly!

the passengers? But later we learned that someone had told him the German ships at that time were little Ritz-Carltons compared to the Union-Castle line, the alternative.

After my life at sea as a deckhand, to travel in supreme comfort was alluring, although I believed that for experience and amusement one should travel steerage, or what is now known as tourist class. But when I hinted it might be a good idea for us to travel hard, as they say in Russia of the third-class, he would have none of 'that sort of nonsense'. He imagined, of course, that travelling steerage was like living in a floating Rowton House (if he had ever heard of such a place) with drunken bums and cheap tarts as fellow-passengers and bug-ridden blankets and the constant threat of yellowjack in the foetid air. He had a further alarming vision of three shabby travellers (members of *his* family) coming down the after-gangplank in Cape Town carrying their own baggage. The idea of travelling light was reasonable, he agreed, though I knew that he was not prepared to consider even this suggestion seriously because it would cut out superintended visits to his tailor for our tropical kit, an item which formed an important factor in his grand plan.

When I realized everything to the last detail had already been arranged I could not resist the suggestion that we might take mink-lined sleeping bags for the veldt, and his 'brows darkened and his eyes flashed lightning'. In a wild effort to placate him I offered one of my cigars but, not unnaturally, he preferred his own.

We learned later that he had already gone down to Southampton to inspect our accommodation; he had, of course, been right about the ship. There was none of the indifference of the old-time stewards in British ships, who still looked on ice in a drink as a strange American custom which must be crushed—the custom, not the ice—at source.

I had spent so much time abroad that I hardly knew the twins. It was generally agreed that they had been grossly spoiled by Mother. Nothing was ever denied them. At Downside they would never have seen their time out had they not cast their magic spell over Father Trafford; it was not only their dark eyes and good looks that accomplished this, but a natural charm they exercised with astonishing results. They had an acute sense of humour, and I soon learned they could hold their drinks and their tongues equally well; but in my eyes their greatest virtue was a kindness, common to both. People are inclined to look on twins as one and inseparable, but I soon learned that Ambrose and Godfrey were characters, each in his own right.

Mother, not Father, came to Southampton to see us off, laden with flowers and yet another suitcase with towels and the spare handkerchiefs she had embroidered with our initials. By the time our gear was assembled (which she helped us to count) we had between us eight cabin trunks, two guncases, two golf bags, and the many strange odds and ends that were said to be Godfrey's photographic equipment. Mother was always irritable when she was seeing off anyone she loved. The more she loved them the crosser she became. When seeing us off to school her sorrow and anxiety had always manifested itself in this unusual way, so we were used to it and loved her all the more as, at the bottom of the gangplank, we hugged her and said good-bye.

As I was busy writing (à la Proust) I kept to my cabin, but I could hardly dodge the fancy-dress ball. As a boy I had always wanted to look like D'Artagnan; but as I grew up my interest in costume waned.

Dick Rawlinson, my playwright brother-in-law, contemptuous of the conventional white satin pierrot motley with its white satin catsuit and black pom-poms, went to a ball dressed as Christopher Columbus. He had taken enormous trouble to have his props and garments historically correct in every detail, as he was courting my sister Ailsa at the time and wished to make a brave show. Under his arm he carried a globe of the world; this was in fact a balloon and not unnaturally it was punctured by a lighted cigarette early in the evening. Because of his height, however, good looks and splendid appearance, to his astonishment he was awarded first prize and announced, not as the great navigator, but as George Villiers, 1st Duke of Buckingham.

As I dressed for this tedious occasion I thought of a limerick we enjoyed as children:

There was a young man called Hall
Who went to a fancy dress ball.
He went, just for fun,
As a halfpenny bun
But the dog ate him up in the hall.

And I thought of the old Chelsea Arts Ball, the balls at Covent Garden and the Quatz Arts in Paris (when one could get a ticket) where I usually wore nothing more exciting than a purple domino with a gold buckle and chain under the black velvet collar.

In those days in Paris it was customary at the *bals masqués* for the women to remain masked until midnight. One New Year's Eve at the Paris Opera House (with my usual luck) I suddenly felt a small cool hand slipped into mine. Through the mask, brilliant eyes gleamed at me and I knew she must be beautiful. She led me to a *loge* where, though I expected her to be greeted by her friends, we were alone.

Level with us and above us the boxes rose tier on tier, each a *cabinet particulier*, glowing darkly red and mysteriously shadowed by tasselled curtains. Below the dancers waltzed and swayed in the glittering horseshoe to the music of a hundred strings. Looking down on them, as they were swirled into a whirlpool of colour, it was as though each couple were flowers in a vast revolving *boutonnière*, lace-bordered and windblown.

In spite of the, alas, uncompromising masculinity of my appearance, I am not without some femininity in my intuitions. Not for one glittering second of self-delusion could this charming creature fool me into thinking she was the wanton she wanted me to believe; the sweet, tipsy perfume of her breath and her reckless determination to enjoy herself at all costs masked, like her face, the reason for her presence there with me, alone and unattended; but I was always conscious of another male, although invisible, presence. When she looked into my eyes it was into someone else's eyes she was looking. When she listened to me mine was another voice, and when she held my hand it belonged to another. I was in no mood for that universal game 'Let's Pretend', and had no wish either to act as a stand-in for someone she loved, or be the instrument of a revenge. Before the midnight bell-strokes had died my Cinderella had flown, leaving no more than the faint perfume of violets on my shoulder where her head had rested.

I didn't try to find her because she had never really been with me. I hoped she'd gone to where she'd come from or where she wished to be, with someone she loved, where we should all be at the beginning of any New Year.

A few months later I was dining in Auteuil with a man (a member of the *bourse*, whom I had only recently met) and his wife. For no particular reason, but because the conversation drifted that way, I told them briefly of the charming New Year's Eve I had spent at the *Bal de L'Opera*; though for me it was still as meaningless and elusive as a dream.

As I said farewell to these new friends my hostess whispered to me: 'You didn't tell us the girl you met was wearing violets in her hair.'

I retain no such fragrant memories of the *Maskenball* aboard the *Ubena*; and made no further public appearance until at long last we arrived in Cape Town. Our suite was ready for us at the Mount Nelson, a Victorian caravanserai built for the comfort of the British Raj, brother-hotel to the Galle-Face in Colombo, the Raffles at Singapore and the Taj Mahal in Bombay. It was designed in the shape of a cross with a nave to the east, which was the restaurant, presided over by a cadaverous English head-waiter, who pounced on me like a cat, giving short, sharp orders to a litter of native under-cats who each answered to the call of 'boy' regardless of age. I received no answer when I called 'waiter!', so ingrained was this colonial custom; but it was a long time before I could bring myself to call 'boy!' to a man old enough to be my father.

Soon a guide—hired by Father, and part of his impeccable planning—introduced himself. He started off rather well, but gradually his information became more and more at variance with that of my guidebook so I paid him off. He had, however, shown us a statue of Cecil Rhodes and here, our duty done and his contract fulfilled, we parted; to his entire satisfaction as he had also been pre-paid by Father.

As advised by my kindly friend, Rudyard Kipling, we drove to Muizenburg. It was one of the places in the Cape he loved most. On the gently shelving sands we watched the Indian Ocean in long rolling combers unfurl itself like a gigantic blue and white flag. Here I made an attempt at surfing, but no matter what I did the board was clearly my master and remained in command throughout the proceedings. It threw me sideways when I wanted to go ahead, it flung me into the air, with vicious kicks, then slammed me down and barked my shins, and didn't forget to clip me sharply on the side of the head as finally and contemptuously it flung me off.

On the Simonstown road we paused at the little cottage (where it was said, Rhodes had drunk himself into the grave) and we stood at the southernmost point of Africa where the two great oceans, Atlantic and Indian, met, and where tides and winds fight forever. We built a cairn and wedged a tree-branch into it; and here I hoisted my shirt. Even Hawes and Curtis would have been proud to see its silken tails pinned to the sky against an angry African sunset by an even angrier wind.

Tiring of Rhodes, that night in Cape Town I trod the lower section of the town amid pungent odours of stew and chilli; and the magnificent African smells blew, like Shakespeare's love, 'where the wind blows', and there were the fumes of ship's tobacco, the reek of cheap perfume. Old excitements of my seagoing days assailed me. The street lamps threw lurid fans of light at each intersection of the narrow streets; but down the irregular network of alleys the darkness was only occasionally speared by shafts of brilliant yellow from swinging doors momentarily striking the cobblestones and liberating voice-chatter and blare of music from automatic pianos. Dim figures moved silently, lost in the night; and only the occasional silver cat-like gleam of bold eyes and women's voices whispering betrayed them.

Up at the Mount Nelson the whites would be sitting over their after-dinner coffee, playing bridge or discussing Rugby football and *stoep* politics, comfortably insulated from unmentionable realities and the pulsing sensuality of Black Africa.

Hours later I went back to the hotel, now void of everything save stale cigar smoke and hothouse scents, empty chairs and sofas, tables with unwashed glasses, discarded newspapers and well-filled ashtrays. The old African night porter, already my friend, brewed me a pot of tea which I had to drink to please him.

I have always enjoyed the fellowship of those who work by night in the hushed halls and lounges of the great hotels. The night porter is a kindly man; he moves quietly and treads softly; he welcomes company, but he knows discretion and, as good Christians should, performs the corporal works of mercy. At the Gloria in Rio there was a night porter who, on one occasion, not only put me to bed and changed my cuff-links into a clean shirt, but thoughtfully laid a bottle of Alka Seltzer on my bedside table with one glass of pure water and another of its stronger brother.

In a queer kind of way, although looked upon as the lowliest, they are in fact in positions of prime importance: they know the comings and goings of all, a fact well-recognized by the secret services of the world. Once I was leaving the Russian Embassy in London in the company of the naval attaché and his assistant. Addressing the night porter I heard the senior official say in English: 'We'll be back at eleven o'clock.' The man replied in Russian what sounded to me like: 'You'll be back at half-past ten.' I was interested, therefore, when our dinner at the old Kensington Palace Hotel moved to a hurried conclusion at a quarter-past ten and the attaché, glancing at his watch, remarked, 'If you don't mind we'll have to be getting back.' It is well to know who is master, the man or the dog.

One evening, attracted by the pleasantly inviting smell of freshly-cut cucumber and gin, I drifted into a downtown bar in Cape Town. Here I met a young South African who was obviously there for a similar reason. He appeared to be very much at home; he was, in fact, to use that expressive cliché, propping up the bar. In reply to something he said, I foolishly told him I'd like to stand atop Table Mountain, but I'd no intention of going by cable car, nor did I intend footing it. At once he offered to fly me there, so we drove out to his private airfield and took off in his Gypsy Moth. Though I was never to set foot on the Table Mountain I can truthfully boast that I have been up the side of it, because it seemed to me he climbed his plane within a few feet of the face of that great level summit, but just as my stomach was beginning to settle he flung the plane into a sharp turn that threw me painfully against the side of the cockpit.

By the time I had readjusted my safety-belt, which had almost cut through my linen suit, I saw we were flying out to sea. Below us was the harbour, and while I was trying to take a photograph, one of the large Castle ships drifted into the lens. She was heading oceanwards. Suddenly the plane nosedived, leaving my stomach in mid-air, and twisted into a spiral. Then it was I knew I was flying with a slightly drunk madman or a slightly mad drunkard. Thoughts of death possessed me and I felt elation, in a way, because whatever else I am, I am certainly a death-snob. What matters to me is how and where it happens. I don't want to die in a ratepayer's office behind the Town Hall in Wigan. I don't want to be shot to death in a sleezy joint in Panama City or killed by a bicycle on the Promenade des Anglais. I have noted the public lavatory as a particularly unsavoury place in which to expire: death is an important event and if possible should be properly staged; no laughing matter, though to be made as enjoyable as possible for the others concerned.

A dear friend of mine, an exquisite of his generation, was killed by a runaway bus in Notting Hill Gate where he was waiting for a number 31. Nothing could have been more wounding to his dignity—killed on the wrong side of the park, waiting for a bus on its devious route to some deplorable destination. Not much of the majesty of death for him.

In a properly ordered world special people would have special arrangements (V.I.P. style) for signing off. It's clearly in order that soldiers, unaccustomed to being alone, should meet group-death in battle; it is their privilege and duty thus to be 'killed in action'; and one for which they are handsomely paid.

As downwards we spiralled dizzily I thought of Borodin, the great Russian composer, dropping dead at a fancy-dress ball, an ending that would not have appealed to me. At all costs there must be no suggestion of the ridiculous. Herr Adlon, the kindly owner of Berlin's former leading hotel and the gentlest of men, was killed by a drunken soldier who hit him over the head with a bottle from his own cellars.

There is, of course, man's inalienable right to destroy himself and choose the time at his own convenience; though the friends of Gerard de Nerval, the somewhat eccentric French poet, were surprised when he hanged himself with his top hat on: until they realized it was his last gesture of contempt for a life and a society he had found little to his liking.

My momentary elation left me as I became giddily aware that we were no longer heading for our Mother, the sea, but for the deck of the vessel below. I had no wish to be spattered among the deck-chairs and davits; but he pulled out of the dive a split second before we hit and began to circle her at mast-level.

I saw him groping for something, and then with a triumphant yell brandished a bouquet, large and costly. In a flash of cellophane it vanished down a smoke-stack. The passengers were swarming the decks in obvious agitation. My friend was leaning out of the open cockpit in a most dangerous way, waving like mad and signalling me to do the same. We must have circled the ship six times at varying low and alarming levels, each more frightening than the last. Now the mass of passengers were rushing from one side to the other, until a great blast from one or all three of the funnels hinted that the long-suffering captain and crew had had enough.

Twenty minutes later we landed safely on his pocket handkerchief of a field in the Constantia district, where he at once produced a bottle of Nederburg, an excellent wine. Indignation, ever foreign to my nature, began to fade. 'What in the name of all that's good and holy was all that about?' I asked.

'Oh, that,' he said. 'That's how I earn my living.' He raised his glass. 'I wanted you to come particularly. You didn't know, but you were impersonating someone else, you were a sort of stand-in; no one can recognize who's who in a flying helmet. It's kind of smart in these parts for people to say to their friends, "We'll fly over the ship, bunch you with flowers and wish you God-speed." I'm hired to do that but I've got to have someone else with me. The people who hire me are usually too bloody frightened to come themselves.' He laughed. 'So everyone's happy. You've climbed your mountain, got a bottle of wine, and I've earned my cheque.'

'So everyone's happy,' we sang in unison.

With my twin brothers I faltered in the steps of Rhodes until we reached his grave in the wild and barren Matopos. Whatever may now be thought of the motives—lust for gold, dreams of empire—of Rhodes and his fellows, I had arrived at a solid respect for their courage and toughness. They had conquered this alien, intemperate land on horse and foot, fighting their way northwards against man and beast. My own brief encounters with the beasts had been—at least to me—alarming indeed. Night on the veldt did not appeal to me. After travelling by car, an old one supplied by our 'White Hunter' (who might once have been white but certainly was no hunter) we ate an indifferent meal and settled down *al fresco* for the night.

I lay awake wrapped in my sleeping bag among the eerie sounds that herald the approach of night; as the sudden darkness fell the great breathing veldt came to life. Around me grass was being parted in movements cautious and whispering; animals were on the move and the life and death struggle for existence had begun. A low wind had risen carrying the bewildering smell of rotting wood, stifling and musty, but not the comforting mustiness of old books. I was aware of a near and moving shape darker than the night, and for a second I saw a pair of glittering emerald eyes. My ears, danger-quickened, detected the sliding slithering of reptiles going about their scaly business. A breathing silence, a scuffle, a short cough and an angry growl, the heavy breathing of animals locked in a death struggle. Now I smelt the stench of fear and heard the crunch and crack of bone and the rip of living flesh, followed by the lapping of thirsty tongues. Above me in the sleeping trees near the pan there was a rustling and flapping, and against the light of the white African moon I saw the death-grey outline of vultures drowsily patient in their upper branches. I pulled my cape over my head because I had been warned that hyenas will take a running bite at a man's head, or anything that moves; then suddenly, with a chill that raced through my body from head to foot, I heard the roar of a distant lion and I knew this at last was Africa and I was listening to the very heartbeat of the continent.

As dawn came I could make out the silhouettes of many animal heads through a veil of low-lying mist; it was as if their bodies were shrouded in white tulle. In long, cautious lines from every direction the heads were approaching the pan to water—antelope, zebra, giraffe. Each herd had a leader moving forward or waiting until he decided it was safe for all to advance. At the pan wild dogs were splashing about in the water, scuffling and fighting. These were the most vicious and formidable of the vermin—they fought in a pack with all the dedication of kamikaze; even the lions would wait their turn at the water-holes until the brutes had moved on. It was only the storks standing aloof on their single pedestal who seemed unconcerned.

By the time our camp was awake I was ready to sleep, but the civilized smell of morning coffee was on the air, the sun had risen and the game had vanished. I might have enjoyed my coffee more if our white hunter hadn't pointed out the sinister trail a horned viper had left, encircling my body like a noose.

The rest of the day we walked and drove across the veldt,

and the birds rose and the animals fled and fell before the winging guns and the slowly rising rifles. The death bag numbered ten duck for the pot; vermin for the sad human pleasure of killing tallied six hyena, three jackal, eight wild dogs.

Later, at the Bulawayo Club, I gazed with respect at the old, faded photographs of these bearded giants of old who had opened up Rhodesia; but I knew that had I been of their generation I would have waited in Cape Town until they had built the railway.

Looking at Rhodes' grave in the wilderness of rock, I had wondered why he had chosen this isolated place in which to be buried; he is reputed to have said : 'From here a man has a view of the world,' a narrow world in all truth now. He chose it probably because instinctively he knew it was as far north as his dream would take him; and in the vain hope that it was a place to which later generations of his countrymen would make pilgrimage. Kipling had written the epitaph.

His immense and brooding spirit still
Shall quicken and control.
Living he was the land, and dead
His soul shall be her soul.

As Father had planned we had followed his path to this last resting place, where thirty-foot of African rock and earth protected his body from the circling vulture and the prowling hyena. Only worms took their toll.

As always in this harsh land thoughts of death and man's preoccupation with its rituals took possession of me. Poor Rhodes, as immortality-bent as a Pharoah, would have had little sympathy with the death-wishes of a patient of my friend, the late Dr Robert Glass.

She was an elderly widow who lived the life of a recluse in the solitudes of Sydenham, refusing even to have a telephone to connect with the outside world. One day he called upon her to find her most desperately ill. She was lucid enough but she was nearing the end. As they awaited the arrival of a nurse my kindly old friend expressed his admiration of the Victorian bric-a-brac encrusting the room, remarking particularly on the beauty of the aspidistra in the window. The nurse duly came and Dr Glass gave her the necessary instructions and took his leave, arranging to call back in the evening.

Unfortunately, as he set forth for his visit, a great fire broke out in Sydenham (one that was to destroy the Crystal Palace) and every approach to her home was blocked by policemen, firemen, pressmen, fire-engines and hoses. When at last he forced his way to the house the old lady had breathed her last, as they say; and Dr Glass, in due course, signed the death certificate.

The old lady's death had of course been in no way due to the delay in the doctor's visit; but her relatives, whom she detested, began to whisper. The whispers intensified when they learned that Dr Glass was a beneficiary under the terms of her will, and rose to a shrill whine when they read a newspaper headline: HEARSE EXCEEDS SPEED LIMIT.

The deceased had expressed a wish to be buried at sea so as to avoid interment in the family vault, where her husband lay: she'd had enough of him in life and wanted to be as far away from him as possible in death. The driver, in court, explained that he had speeded, not to hasten the obsequies, but so as not to miss the tide at Bexhill where the boating-burial party awaited the coffined corpse.

The relatives scented something very 'fishy' about the doctor's visits, benefits and the subsequent 'rush to the coast'. Dr Glass was visited by the C.I.D. men who, naturally, accepted his explanations and considered the affair closed. They were mistaken. A few days later the old lady reappeared, washed up on the beach at Hastings.

At her next burial she was securely laid in the family vault, where she still lies o'ertopping her husband in death as she did in life; and Dr Glass received a letter from her solicitors asking when it would be convenient for him to take possession of the aspidistra she had willed him.

In the late afternoon we set out for the Victoria Falls. Twenty miles away we could hear the thunder of this mighty waterfall, which I recommend as a spectacle to all who are not hydrophobic. A river the width of Oxford Circus to Marble Arch like a flood of molten silver moves inexorably to the rim of a sheer precipice, to hurl itself into an unfathomed cauldron 400 feet below, its spray fountaining 1,000 feet into the African sky, in a galaxy of multi-coloured rainbows and watershot stars. As a painter

Wilson said of the lesser Tivoli affair: 'Well done, Water, by God!'

In the hotel bar we threw our raincoats down and drank regal whiskies to the memory of Dr David Livingstone and Cecil Rhodes.

CHAPTER IX

Publishing: an occupation for gentlemen?

ANON

Now Barrabas was a publisher

BYRON

A month later I was to lunch with Father at the Carlton Club. As I strolled down St James's Street on a sunny but cold day wearing a light overcoat, I was wondering whether I should order a heavier one from Johns and Pegg, my tailor, friend and financier in times of stress. I had just turned into Pall Mall on the Palace side still pondering this serious matter when suddenly I heard a fierce Irish whisper: 'You're on fire, sor.' There seemed to be no one nearby: then I realized the voice had come from the interior of the sentry-box. 'Saw the smoke a way off, sor,' the guardsman hissed, ventriloquist or prison-style, from the corner of his mouth. I could now smell the burning vegetable substance and then realized I was trailing not clouds of glory but a column of black smoke behind me. Suddenly all became clear. I was more of a guardsman than I knew.

Instinctively on nearing the sentry-box (no officer of the Brigade is supposed to smoke a pipe in the street) and anticipating having to return a salute (guardsmen salute their officers when wearing civilian clothes), I had stuffed the glowing pipe in my pocket before lifting my precariously tilted bowler. Thanks to the sentry's presence of mind tragedy was averted and I was able to extinguish the conflagration without the help of the fire brigade; but my overcoat fell away from me like an ashen shroud.

Thus in a rather intemperate way my destiny or guardian angel had decided the issue for me: the first thing Father said to me on our meeting was: 'It is madness not to wear an overcoat in England. You're not in Cannes now. You'd better go to Leslie and Roberts and order a coat on my account.'

He was in great form, although he had recently suffered a humiliating experience which would have plunged a lesser man into some despair. He had been summoned to serve on a jury for the first and (he hoped) the last time in his life. Being who he was or what he was (he was not certain which) they had elected him foreman. The charge was larceny. Father was convinced the prisoner was innocent; not so the rest of the jury, but persuaded of the justice of his cause it took him more than an hour to win them over to his view. Exhausted, he had hardly done so when the Clerk of the Court walked in announcing that their services would no longer be required, as the man had changed his plea to guilty and had asked for ten other charges to be taken into consideration.

After lunch Father's plans for my future came to light; and assisted by the Cockburns '97 and the Larrañaga Coronas, seemed to me very agreeable. He explained he had bought out the publisher Eveleigh Nash (he hated to be involved in a business which was not under his direct control) and intended carrying on the business under the imprint of Grayson & Grayson. My brother Brian, who was already a director of the company, welcomed me; particularly as they wanted someone to scout for young and promising authors. I wouldn't be enslaved by routine, my expenses would be liberal and I would be expected to continue my own writing. The whole idea was so pleasing I immediately accepted.

Father had set his heart on a delightful old tumble-down house in the City from which we would publish. The address, Ave Maria Lane, not far from Paternoster Row, attracted him. It was off the main thoroughfares, and hard by St Paul's. In Father's mind he saw twilit cloisters, and the mystical props of bell, book and candle. Though in many ways he was a practical man, he loved to indulge his fancy, and he was disappointed when he learned the house was for sale on leasehold only. He had to own a place freehold so that he could alter it in any way he wished: he was a compulsive redesigner, builder and adaptor. Building, renovating and enlarging houses was his hobby and greatest extravagance. I believe, though he would never have admitted it, that he actually loved houses more than he did ships.

It was a disappointed man, therefore, who settled for premises in Curzon Street and the West End instead of the City with its ancient guilds and mediaeval traditions. This alternative house, in style Georgian, was really far more suitable for our purpose; unfortunately it had been at some time renovated. Father called in Sir Albert Richardson, the leading authority on the period. He was given *carte blanche* to return the house to its original design with the necessary adaptations. First he produced a genuine porticoed front door and fanlight. I always wondered what beautiful house he must have pillaged to do this. The door itself was old, black and glossy with a brass knocker to which it had echoed through the decades. Soon an exquisite bow window, delicately carved and jewelled with Georgian glass, bosomed into Curzon Street; and inside the house paint and varnish were stripped to reveal pine panelling of beauty and simplicity.

The professor then chose Georgian light-fittings, door knobs, door-stoppers, etcetera, but it was Father's perfect taste in rugs and carpets that settled the problem of the parquet floors.

Five friends were co-opted into the firm—I cannot call it a business for publishing was then 'an occupation for gentlemen'—and although all were quite diverse they yet shared two things in common: great charm and a total ignorance of the profitable printing and selling of books.

There was carefree Albert Monico, whose father owned a famous restaurant in Piccadilly in the days when it was the hub of fashion and not the haunt of hippies. Richard Hogg was a descendant of Hogg, companion of Shelley's youth. Handsome, blue-eyed Martin Wilson was the son of the great Edwardian *flâneur*, Sir Matthew (Scatters) Wilson. David Tennant, pure Regency, known as 'White' David to distinguish him from his cousin 'Black' David; and Gerald Kearley, now Lord Devenport, who alone had acumen and took the activities with the high seriousness they undoubtedly deserved. The unfortunate Mr Taylor, Father's secretary, acted as financial watchdog.

The boardroom had four long french windows overlooking the Public Schools' Club, with a glimpse of Green Park down Bolton Street. In this room there was a visitors' book handily placed between two cut-glass ship's decanters engraved *Outward* on one and *Homeward* on the other. Father liked anyone visiting the house to be suitably entertained, and the privilege was seldom abused particularly, as the Madeira was excellent but not to everyone's taste. It would have been a different story had it been whisky or gin, but Father insisted on nothing but this old, sweet wine which (as perhaps he knew) gave me an instant headache. It was not long, therefore, before I had established sub-offices in the Curzon Hotel bar opposite, the Washington bar next to Trumper's (the world's most famous barber who used to visit Buck House three times a week to trim the Monarch's whiskers) and Dirty Dick's, the pub across the street.

It was thus with great hopes that I began a career as publisher's scout—with the run of my teeth and money in the bank—working in an interesting world peopled by creative fellow-creatures. It was as though there was a gardenia for my buttonhole every day of the week, in the manner of my godfather, Stanley Stubbs, a partner in Scrimgours, the stockbrokers, who wore a fresh carnation every day from the age of 21 until his 71st birthday, celebrating which he died: it could be reckoned roughly in his lifetime that he had spent £1,500 on this pleasure and adornment.

As soon as I had taken over my delightful Georgian table so friendly and undesk-like, I went in search of my old friend from Berlin days, Pat Kirwan. This was no easy quest—he might be in London, Berlin or Dublin. Someone had seen him here, someone there; as I walked in by one door it seemed that he had only just left by the other. Pat had a remarkable flair for knowing what was going on in the underworld of talent striving to assert itself. I myself had been away from London and had lost touch with the literary world.

In the opera *Il Tabarro*, a murder has just been committed on a barge in the Seine. At the height of a most passionate situation a delightful guide appears quite suddenly on the quayside above the barge, followed by a party of tourists to whom he points out the beauties of Paris in a cool metallic tenor. In the third act of *La Bohème* Mimi lies dying to the accompaniment of deathless music, while Gustave sings a long farewell to the beloved overcoat he must pawn to buy cough medicine. And similarly while I was engaged in this unremitting search for Pat interruptions of the most delightful kind often halted my mission.

Day after day I left Brook Street early, alone and unarmed, determined to comb the mysterious hinterland of St John's Wood, where studios and love-nests abounded. Failing there I contemplated quartering the dangerous bedsitter district crouching between Swiss Cottage to the north, Camden Town to the east, and Kilburn to the west. As a last resort I resolved even to range that unending axis of misfortune, Goldhurst Terrace, of which it is said that with the exception of Siberia and certain suburbs of Stockholm its suicide rate is without compare.

Already exhausted after following a useless trail in Albany Street I was contemplating the heights of Primrose Hill, when I was spotted by a man I knew sufficiently well to accept his kind invitation to luncheon. It was only when he told me that he had reserved a table at the London Zoological Society (of which he was a member—a distinction he shares with Sean Treacy, the literary landlord of the Queen's Elm) that I regretted having accepted, particularly when he promised to show me the lions being fed.

As the reader may have realized, wild animals were not my line of country, either free on the veldt or safe behind bars. Once I'd been to the Hamburg Zoo by chance; but the Bronx Zoo I had visited by design only because I wanted to see the place where Caruso, the greatest of all tenors, had been arrested for pinching a woman's bottom.

After a splendid luncheon I felt it would be churlish to refuse to visit the lions in their den, but nothing depressed me more than the sight of these noble creatures (in addition there were leopards, panthers and other species of the wild cat) pacing up and down in lifelong captivity in the confines of their horrible cages. At the first opportunity I slipped away and entered the more congenial and friendly atmosphere of the monkey house. The inmates of these commodious cages were jumping, skipping and swinging in interrupted ecstasy to a chattering screeching and squawling cacophony. Here at least there was the same semblance of enjoyment as in a school playground. Indeed I was welcomed with a sort of reception normally accorded only to the Captain of Games.

It was while I was watching the antics of a small group of monkeys on the high swings, that I first felt my eyes being drawn irresistibly to a figure opposite me on the far side of the vast cage. As I looked across, a pair of heavy-lidded eyes flickered and our eyes met through the bars. Immediately I realized it was someone I knew; but there was more to it than that.

The man was an eminent magistrate in whose house I had once dined and wined: fortunately at the time I didn't realize that the very next morning I was to appear before him on a minor motoring offence. He fined me thirty shillings; but as I was never invited to his house again I assumed that those who incurred his displeasure from the bench could no longer expect the hospitality of his board.

He was standing like something screwed to the floor, motionless except for one hand fingering a watch chain tightly stretched across his imposing belly; his whole bearing reflected a most sober approach to life. He was clad legally in black Homburg, black coat and striped trousers, and carried a neatly rolled umbrella and a copy of *The Times* tucked under his arm. I was quite moved by the expression of happy concentration in his shrewd blue eyes as he watched the little animals. Then one of them suddenly swung across my line of vision executing, possibly for our mutual entertainment, a double somersault like the man on the flying trapeze. As the monkey landed between us, once more our eyes met and were transfixed. There was something unbecoming about our encounter, so I looked away; but even with our eyes disengaged our ears had still to share the pandemonium and chattering disputatious squalling of the little animals as they sprang from their haunches up to the swings. I might have enjoyed watching them hanging and swinging by hands and arms and tails had I not been so acutely conscious of the unmoving and splendid legal figure on the opposite side of the cage.

It seemed to me that this ludicrous situation, each staring at the other through the bars, would never end. It was as if one of us was in durance and the other a kind of prison visitor.

For one merciful moment we were screened from one another by an ape who seemed to be the leader of his group; but quickly he scampered away and once more our eyes met and were locked.

It was only by summoning all my forces that I was able to drag my gaze away from his and hasten to the exit. From a safe distance I looked back and saw that he was wiping his forehead with a handkerchief like a man who had met with more than he bargained for.

But the aching question persisted, what was this unsmiling man up to? What rule of action, procedure or principle of conduct was this man, with his vast knowledge of the law, studying in the uninhibited department of life? I could find no answer, and hurried away to continue my search.

At last I heard a rumour that Pat had been seen in Earls Court. In the twenties and thirties (before it became part of the Australian outback) Earls Court was still clinging to the relics of old decency and had about it an air of seedy respectability. It was said that if you went into any pub in the Earls Court Road and asked the barmaid, 'Has the Major been in yet?' she would smile and say: 'Not yet, sir, but he's bound to be in later if you care to wait.' I decided that a modified application of the same technique might bring me closer to the heels of my elusive friend whom, as I have said, I had last met with in pre-Hitler Berlin, from whence he had fled to escape the attention of Stalin's secret police. I knew from experience that O.G.P.U. operated pretty widely, but it puzzled me that he should still be hiding here in London, a tuppenny tube ride from Westminster, the Fount of Liberty itself.

The Earls Court Road is long and its pubs many but I was in no wise dismayed. I was on a pub crawl with a purpose, which made a nice change, as they say. And at last, in a lounge with wicker chairs, glass-topped tables and browning palm fronds sprouting limply from china pots there was evidence of my man. I had whispered my question to the barmaid: 'Has Mr Patrick Kirwan been in yet?'

Over the mahogany a porcelain smile flashed from a cupid's bow. 'I don't think I know a gentleman of that name, sir,' she replied gently.

Then, uneasily, I became aware of the customer standing next to me at the bar. He was a ponderous kind of man whose every movement seemed the result of long deliberation. He wore a bowler hat and was possessed of a briefcase. He raised his whisky glass and I knew his eyes were swivelled at me over the rim. I was 'under observation'. He set down his glass and, after some long, slow, inward process that made the term 'reflection' seem somehow trivial, he addressed me softly, reproach in his voice.

'Excuse me—but I couldn't help overhearing your question.'

'I tried to make it discreet,' I replied a little defiantly.

'Even so, sir—don't you think it's best left to us?'

This didn't sound to me like the Russian O.G.P.U. What was he? A bum-bailiff? A writ-server? Not from what I knew of them; mine had all been humble men who drank in the four-ale bar and certainly not costly whisky amid the splendour of wicker chairs and potted palms.

'A false move now and just when I'm getting a lead and he'll be off God knows where. We don't want that now—do we, sir?' I looked at his boots. Large. A policeman?

'We certainly don't,' I replied.

'He's what you'd call elusive.'

'You can say that again.' I was beginning to feel like a partner in a cross-talk act devised by some Kafka of the music halls: what the devil was it all about?

'You've no need to tell me who you are, sir. Your question over the bar told me at once. It's my job to put two and two together.' I nodded agreement at this.

'I'm waiting here for my contact,' he continued. 'He's another Mick—very cagey. I wouldn't like him to see you—might carry information back—so if you wouldn't mind. . . .'

'You want me to go!'

Now he nodded. 'Yes. It's best to leave it entirely to us—most injured parties do.'

At this I made a fast and most convincingly conspiratorial exit—and laughed myself silly all the way to the public bar. Pat was in close hiding sure enough, but not from O.G.P.U. He was evading a private eye enlisted by a posse of cuckolded husbands, for one of whom I'd been mistaken. Now from behind the dividing screen, I myself had the private eye 'under observation'.

About the identity of the 'contact' who presently joined him there could be no confusion. He was a 'Mick', all six feet of him: grey-haired, square-shouldered—and unmistakably ex-guardsman. The 'dick' entertained him lavishly, spoke to him earnestly and, on parting, shook him by the hand, pressing monies into his palm. From the four-ale doorway I watched the sleuth buy his ticket in the Underground and vanish below; then hurried to confront the 'contact'.

He greeted me pleasantly as a fellow Irish guardsman when I told him my name—at that time my brother Tristram was Colonel of the Regiment—and was even more delighted when he learned I was a friend in search of Pat who, he said, was lodging in the house of which he and his wife were caretakers.

When I hinted that I didn't like the company he'd just been keeping he began to laugh. Mr Kirwan knew all about that—he was keeping an eye on the fellow for him, and he was under instructions to betray Mr Kirwan's whereabouts at the next meeting. Mr Kirwan hadn't made up his mind yet whether your man should be given the address of a whorehouse in Paris or a dry-out for drunks run by Trappist monks in Tipperary. It was evident that he fully shared Pat's peculiar sense of humour.

Craftily and tortuously he conducted me to the lodging house, a kind of tall cliff-dwelling in a terrace off the Earls Court Road, and *en route* told me that Pat's presence there was not only the cause but the result of some confusion. The house was owned by the widow of a famous Anglo-Irish general, and the old lady, a little astray in the head, was busy in the affairs of an Irish Loyalists' Association founded to give comfort to landlords of the Ascendancy who had left Ireland and their estates when the Irish gained their independence. On Pat presenting himself there looking for a lodging, and on hearing his name, she had insisted that he was one of the Kirwans of Castle Hackett, in flight from some Connaught *jacquerie*, with his horses and cattle maimed, his crops destroyed and his ancestral home in flames. She had insisted that he be given refugee status, three pairs of bedsocks and the largest room in the house, with the ex-guardsman as a batman thrown in.

Pat was, of course, in bed, working on a book which we were to publish later and which brought him a *succès d'estime* under the title of *Black Exchange*. No man I have ever known has spent more time in bed, either at work or play, or quite simply conserving his energies. Never having lived in Earls Court I was surprised at the magnificent view from his room. I had seen most of the famous glaciers in Norway and in Switzerland but none surpassed the magnificent sight that greeted me as it rose from Pat's very window sill. Here was reflected from a thousand facets every variation of colour by day and colour by night known to man. I leaned from the window spellbound at the vision of the great sweeping arc of glass that spanned the Earls Court Station, supported within a delicate lacework of girders. It is conceivable that a man might tire of Earls Court, but of the dome of Earls Court Station, surely never.

When I asked him how he fared, he broke into the same old lovely lament, 'The Famine Song'; and his grand baritone must have surely penetrated and brought comfort to a thousand surrounding bedsitters bending over their little gasrings; and even the ticket collectors under the great glacier must have pricked up their ears with pleasure, ears still appreciative and perceptive, because it was in the days before the onslaught of radio, transistors and piped melodies. Judging the form from the song we drove to the Ritz for luncheon where we entered into a conspiracy to hijack every promising writer in search of a publisher.

It could be said of Pat that wherever he put his lips to the glass he certainly had his ear to the ground; and so it came to pass I was soon moving in a world of poets and pimps, writers and publicans. Books of all sorts were like people of all sorts. Readers care what happens and a book either entertains or bores; I also learned that to be a successful publisher, apart from having a small gold-mine from which to draw, a man must love the books he publishes and he must be prepared to support writers ungrudgingly through hard times; he must be a business man to deal with printers and binders (to say nothing of agents); he must have a genius for spotting talent and an instinct for sensing genius; and a thirst for the company of writers; he must, in fact, be a combination of Rothschild, Job, Diaghilev and Bacchus.

CHAPTER X

Our ship hath touched upon the desarts of Bohemia
[Exit, pursued by a bear].

SHAKESPEARE

In spite of our rather amateur status in publishing we soon attracted a list of authors under the Tudor Rose, our house sign, more than worth a second glance. It included among others François Mauriac, Algernon Blackwood, Liam O'Flaherty, Francis Stuart, Edgar Lee Masters, Percy Wyndham Lewis, Ilya Ehrenbourg, Drieu la Rochelle and Colette, a well-diversified company. Pat and I persuaded Frank Budgen, painter and friend of James Joyce, to write an account of their friendship in Switzerland. *James Joyce and the Making of Ulysses* was the first really intimate account of the famous Irishman and his work during a time when *Ulysses* was still banned in England and America, and of course in Ireland.

Once, while Joyce was looking through the proof sheets, they kept slipping from his knees; he said to Frank, 'Galley proofs remind one of the persons of the Trinity—get a good hold of one and you lose your grip of the others.' As Joyce read on he said: 'I never knew you could write so well—it must be your association with me.' This was a unique work, the forerunner of a hundred lesser books on the great Irish writer.

We published *The Long Journey* by Johannes V. Jenson, which was followed by a beautifully written historical novel, *The Fall of the King*, which Pat Kirwan translated; this great Danish writer, then comparatively unknown, was later awarded the Nobel Prize for Literature.

Our plan of campaign, if it can be described as planning, was to drift about those bohemian circles where one was most likely to meet writers in search of a publisher or in search of a more sympathetic publisher; this method was far more in keeping with my way of life, and far more pleasing than standing on literary agents' doorsteps waiting for the scraps that fell from the rich publishers' tables: the dog that runs around is the one who finds the bone. *J'avais la clef des champs*: the key was in the gate.

Thus we moved in on the world (and underworld) of writers, musicians and artists, all with their golden dreams. This was the London equivalent of the *fin du siècle*, the Parisian twilight of Baudelaire, Verlaine and Rimbaud. It was as if we were in a similar shadowy undergrowth of woods shot with an occasional ray of sunshine, and from which some paths led to fame and others to death.

The literary scene was a strange one in many respects. There were the bestseller novelists who lived on the hilltops high above the dark forest. Many of them had staked territorial claims, unregistered but jealously guarded. Hugh Walpole had, for instance, taken over the Lake District. He was a writer of great popularity, with a great ambition to be the G.O.M. of English letters; and he might have achieved it had not Somerset Maugham ridiculed him in *Cakes and Ale*. They were old enemies, having quarrelled over a good-looking waiter in Florence.

There were, of course, the critics. Some unofficially reading for publishers, for whom they officially could be very influential. They were to be seen creeping to clandestine conferences with their masters; but there were also the uncompromised but lean men-of-letters lugging their review copies to the second-hand booksellers; publishers had learned it was unkind and unwise to stamp books 'review copy' and thus decrease their re-sale price. Arnold Bennett had a page in the *Evening Standard* where he concentrated his praises on one book: he had the distinction and responsibility of being able to create overnight one bestseller once a week. Happily the literary cocktail party to launch a book had not been thought of, but a similar idea must have already been germinating in Christina Foyle's lovely dark head.

There was little room for me in the galaxy; but I had conceived a character called 'Gun Cotton', who was not without a faithful following. Powys Mathers, who under the black mask of 'Torquemada' used to torture his *Observer* victims with the cruellest crossword in the country, was particularly kind about him and described him as 'head and shoulders my favourite Secret Service Agent'. For recreation and as a form of penance he composed witty and erudite erotic verse (he had also translated *The Arabian Nights*). He foiled the police and Joynson-Hicks by issuing them as 'renderings' from the Chinese or Swahili, as fancy took him.

Ralph Straus, of the *Sunday Times*, used to give me good notices. He was an excellent novelist himself and also an old Harrovian, so I always suspected there was a little of the 'old pals act' in his reviews.

Ralph Strauss, of the *Sunday Times*, used to give me good I was strolling down Piccadilly in 'full rig' of morning dress, grey topper and racing glasses when he hailed me as he came out of his club.

'Been to a wedding, Rupert?' he cried cheerily.

'Good Lord, no, Ralph,' I said. 'I've just come back from Ascot.'

'Ascot,' he mused. 'Of course. That's *flat-racing*, isn't it?'

At that time Boots' lending library was enormously important and when Mr Richardson's initial order for my own books reached 600 copies it was safe to print a first edition of 5,000. The unkindest notice of *Scarlet Livery*, my first book and probably the most honest, was that of an old Fleet Street friend who explained blandly: 'I had to encourage you to do better next time.' An acquaintance crossed the street to tell me he'd read it. 'There's one thing that puzzled me,' he said. 'Please tell me,' I broke in eagerly. He was candid. 'I can't understand why you ever wrote it,' he said. Publishing was a complicated game to play unless you knew all the players, all the unwritten rules and all the gambits.

Brian had chosen a small team of readers whose views on life, love and letters in course of time one learned to know; often we could guess their reactions to certain manuscripts and we could thus ring the changes. We paid three guineas for reading and reporting on a manuscript, which was probably more than most publishers paid at that time, but in building up a good list we regarded this as money well-invested; no reader's report was regarded as final until it had been read by at least one of us in the firm. Our readers were people who were fully 'alive and around'; only the occasional manuscript was sent to the retired don in the university city or the proverbial and improvident old vicar in Cornwall.

Under the title of Grayson Books we published in limited editions works by James Hanley, John Collier, Arthur Calder-Marshall, A. E. Coppard, Patrick Kirwan, Graham Greene, H. E. Manhood, T. F. Powys, Rhys Davis. We smuggled Liam O'Flaherty through the Jonathan Cape lines and shanghaied him on to a cargo boat. Cunningly we supplied him with reams of foolscap to allay his boredom; thus he was driven to write an autobiography, *Shame the Devil*, a frank, revealing book which embodied one of this great Irish writer's best short stories.

Meetings with Liam were usually at the Cadogan Arms, which was Augustus John's local near Mallord Street, where John had a studio house—later when Gracie Fields bought it I used to visit there with her friend John Flanagan, the portrait painter. Here she used to entertain her friends to dinner which, however elaborate, was always referred to in Lancashire fashion as high tea.

For some reason most of our authors and would-be authors preferred to meet us in pubs rather than at the office. O'Flaherty once told me how he had rather unwillingly gone down to Clouds to meet T. E. Lawrence, with that great *homme de lettres* Edward Garnett. At his sixteenth-century cottage they had been given a very half-hearted welcome, and when Liam put his hand on the enormous oak beam that supported the ceiling and probably the entire building, Lawrence remarked: 'That's strong enough to take the weight of a man hanging by his neck.'

Liam, anxious to escape from the strained and alcoholically dry atmosphere, thereupon suggested they should go over to the local inn. Without replying Lawrence left the room and a few minutes later the drowsy Dorset air was shattered by the death-rattle of his motorcycle.

This was before Richard Aldington, author of that better than bestseller *Death of a Hero*, had written his book on Lawrence, pointing out inaccuracies, improbabilities and impossibilities in his work and disclosing for the first time Lawrence's illegitimacy. I used to meet Aldington at lunch at a pub opposite the church of St Martin's-in-the-Fields which for some unknown reason he

Sir Henry Grayson, Knight of the British Empire, Member of Parliament, High Sheriff of Anglesey, Commissioner of St John of Jerusalem, Commendatore della Coronna d'Italia, Officier de la Legion d'honneur, Commander of the Order of Leopold

Sir Hugh Walpole in his Laurel Canyon home

Merle Oberon would catch sharks, but never anything smaller than herself

seemed to like. The book received a most unfavourable reception and he felt very strongly that he had been ill-treated by the critics and the public. Every writer knows that a biographical work can take a different course, as research, like the merciless lens of the camera, reveals the truth. What he hadn't taken into account was that Lawrence was a national hero.

Percy Wyndham Lewis, the author of that superb satirical work *The Apes of God*, was a difficult fish to play. The expression 'highbrow' had just filtered into England from America like a deadly virus, together with its natural adjunct 'lowbrow'. It was eagerly seized upon by the English, who adore classifications; but Percy, a man of original thought and a master of language, the great brim of his black hat pulled well down, was browless, unidentifiable and dangerous.

At our first meeting he examined me in his jade-cold way as though I were a specimen from another world. I was a microbe new to him and what he didn't know he didn't understand, and because he didn't understand he was uneasy. He was a man essentially interested as much in behaviour as in ideas; he had no use for the romantic bourgeois, such as myself, so I was acutely conscious of the scrutiny behind his soft voice and gentle manner, and it reminded me immediately and uncomfortably of an encounter with an apparently friendly Customs and Excise officer in search of contraband.

Such knowledge as I had of the world had been hammered out of experience by reading the great books and sailing the great seas; but Percy's reasoning was born of his icy brain; his thoughts were scions of the ferocious, frigid aristocracy of his mind and his writing like his drawings was chisel-cold in its clarity. However, I was too anxious to secure *The Apes of God* for our list to be afraid of his calculating eyes (treacherous minions of his mind) or his biting tongue; nor could I go in fear of a man who was himself so afraid of the market place.

Norman Douglas had described James Joyce's *Ulysses* as 'too excremental for his taste', but Percy had been a friend of Joyce too long to let him off so lightly, so he dismissed the masterpiece as 'a monumental diarrhoea'.

'I have always thought it would solve many problems if English painters were born blind.' At these his words, a whisper must have started in the abode of the Gods to echo through the vaulted caverns: 'So be it; but first let *this* great draughtsman complete his best work.' Darkness came upon Lewis in the years before his death.

He had written a piece on Hemingway entitled *The Dumb Ox*, condemning his anti-intellectualism. Sylvia Beach, of the Shakespeare Bookshop in the Rue de l'Odéon, should have known better than to show it to Ernest, because he was not the sort of writer or man who liked to be described as a 'proletarian clown and a pseudo-lumberjack'. She suffered the fate of all bearers of ill-tidings. Fortunately the only china the American 'brute male' bull-writer could find to break in the shop was one green bowl containing one yellow tulip.

I suppose in some way most men gifted with the highest intelligence (as was Lewis) must of necessity be sick men: to have given up all hope for the human race is not conducive to health. No pardoner could have been meaner with his indulgences, and laughter without the undersong of kindness can ring as hollow as a tomb.

As a cloak-and-dagger intellectual he will surely never be equalled—much less surpassed. His office-cum-studio was at that time, despite the revealing name, in Percy Street. Strategically situated between Stulic's Eiffel Tower Restaurant, Kleinfeld's Fitzroy Tavern and The Plough in Museum Street, it was ideal for observation and listening, an advance post, as it were, for the enemy behind enemy lines.

This sealed, locked, padlocked, bolted, enchained hideout was equipped rather than furnished with two well-screwed-up packing cases (for the occasional use of guest or model), an easel and a sinister black steel-braced trunk pressed into a shadowy corner of the room and, for greater security, clamped to the floor. I never saw the second room. It could have been graced, for all I knew, with Louis XV pieces standing on Aubusson carpets and with walls hung in damask. Only one thing was certain: it contained a utensil of sorts, because when he disappeared therein one could hear the tinkle-tinkle one associates with a male person peeing into a tin can; and that during this time I was conscious of one cold eye watching me closely through an ill-concealed peep-hole. It was probably the only time he and I saw eye to eye.

I was never quite sure whether his appearance was contrived or whether, like mist on the Welsh mountain, it was an act of

God. Was it caution as he descended the stairs or affectation in the hall that made him heave on his cumbersome overcoat, wedge his hat down, smother his neck in a thick, dark muffler, grope for the latch with heavily gloved fingers; then step into the summer-hazy street. He was extremely tall in a bulky, shapeless way, easily recognizable in volume yet strangely difficult to observe in detail; you had to be satisfied with the overall impression of a man muffled up beyond the normal state of muffledom, like a figure emerging from a London fog, or an apparition stepping out of a *drozhki* in a strange place at midnight under a misty winter's moon in Russia. Day or night, indoors or outdoors, he seemed to be most comfortable when he was wearing his black halo of a hat, a great wheel that had slipped a cog and landed on the horn-rimmed glasses masking the thoughts behind the pale face. When he was amused his smile was not without radiance, but it came with the unexpectancy of a cork popping from a bottle of still champagne. Unfortunately this happened very rarely when he was with me, because we enjoyed a different kind of laughter. Good-hearted people and those who enjoyed his friendship (all temporarily) like Pound, Joyce, Eliot and Ford Madox Ford have assured us (and they were all honest men) that he had an acute sense of humour, though I suspect it was not of the infectious variety. Mentally, of course, I couldn't play his game; but it annoyed him that he couldn't play mine; we were ill-matched as opponents for the game we had on hand. He would turn up with fives gloves (he was a great glove man) and I would be there with a squash racket. In spite of these differences we eventually came to an understanding, blessings on his head, and we published *The Apes of God* and later a magnificent travel book, the only one he ever wrote, *Filibusters in Barbary*.

One day he was swaying over me, his favourite stance, laying down the law, criticizing Shaw, another tall man, with whom he had some spiritual dealings whose nature he never disclosed to me. Just to be tiresome I reminded him of the old adage, 'Tall men can be like tall houses—their upper stories can be often rather sparsely furnished.' Once when he announced he was off to buy a new hat to replace the mildewed specimen he was sporting I suggested: 'You'd look good in a black one, green doesn't suit you.' Invariably he gave as his address the Pall Mall Safe Deposit, and when I remarked, naturally without any intention of hurting his feelings, rather indeed as a compliment, 'A big man like you must find it rather cramped in there', he wasn't amused.

One evening I ran into him at the Breevort in New York. His hat was pulled over his eyes even more than usual and he had all the appearance of a Russian anarchist (circa 1907). We did the rounds of the speakeasies together, for we seemed to belong one to the other like the two diverse sides of one coin. At one of the cellar-bars we encountered an uncomfortably inquisitive cell of young intellectuals. They naturally wanted to know who Percy was, because however exaggerated his appearance there was always about his person an aura of authority. Anyway his conversation alone singled him out from other men. I told them that he had edited and largely written and published (in his own good time) a number of literary periodicals, *Blast*, *The Enemy*, *The Vorticist*; he had written *Tarr*, *Childermass* and *The Apes of God*.

'*The Apes of God*,' one of the young men echoed enthusiastically, extending his hand to Percy, 'then you must be Osbert Sitwell.' I left the party quickly, hoping he'd forget I was ever there. I was in trouble enough without being present to overhear this sort of remark. In my casual way I had already unintentionally penetrated his defences, even unto the citadel; thus I was ripe for the stab in the back, the glass of poisoned wine or a burst from the Lewis gun. I was soon to realize it could be dangerous to feed grapes to a tiger.

Someone once said: 'I can handle my enemies but save me from my friends.' It should have been a Sitwell, for of all Percy's 'friends' none suffered more from his biting pen. Edgell Rickward, because he was a brilliant poet and possibly because he was the kindest of men, was cruelly lampooned under the name of Wreckword. Dick Wyndham, a fellow-painter and erstwhile disciple-patron, suffered too; but he was a match for Percy. He retaliated, aiming his arrows with great accuracy where they hurt Percy most. To the great artist's consternation insertions started appearing in the agony column of *The Times* offering FOR SALE *original drawings by Percy Wyndham Lewis, one pound or nearest offer*. Dick Wyndham, being a wealthy dilettante and a man of generous impulses, had bought a large number of Percy's works in order to help him through a difficult time.

For ten days Percy sulked in one of his hideouts, emerging from his fastness only in the grey dawn, when he crept along the by-ways to Printing House Square to purchase with trembling hands and peruse with glassy eye the first edition of *The Times*. Dick had arranged with cunning for the advertisements to appear intermittently, the better to prolong the torture, as a sadist-dentist artfully withdraws the drill to lull his patient into a sense of security before returning to the attack and driving the needle into the very root of the poor bugger's nerve. Percy in his wisdom must have known that neither God nor Dick would give a man a burden heavier than he could bear; but he must learn humility and proclaim it. If he did it must have been in the subdued tones of the confessional, because no one else heard it. There must have been some sort of *détente* because the advertisements ceased and Percy reverted thankfully to his awkward and accustomed way of life.

It was a curious preoccupation that compelled this brilliant but bad-tempered writer, this manipulator of ideas and words (ready to shoot down, like Napoleon, any publisher who disagreed with him), to libel his friends; and when he wasn't libelling them with his pen, to slander them with his tongue. D. H. Lawrence, 'the personal appearance artist', he sneered, was no more than 'a vibration on the eyelash of God', and as an artist 'an incompetent Gauguin'. The Sitwells were a 'circus'. Joyce was 'the poet of the shabby, genteel, impoverished intelligentsia of Dublin'. If he had read Proust's majestic work, *A la Recherche du Temps Perdu*, he wouldn't admit it. Asked his age he replied, 'I'm sticking at 40 till I pass the word around.'

A few years later I too was awarded the ink-black badge of his friendship. He employed his usual weapon, a pen sharpened to dagger point with which he etched my likeness in *Snooty Baronet*, cutting lines jagged and deeper than scars and poisoned with acidic brilliance; it was no joke unless you enjoy being ridiculed. As a friend of mine remarked when asked what he thought of Lewis : 'Very funny if it isn't you.'

We never met again, so I was never to hear his dark laughter at the sweet consummation of his revenge for past irreverences. Because of the force of his intellect he had never been beloved or revered; but at the end he attained the majesty of high tragedy when 'the sea mists enveloped him' and blindness imprisoned him in its darkness. He had been betrayed by those observant eyes, but never by his indomitable courage. As night descended who can forget his last challenge to life. 'Pushed into an unlighted room,' he wrote, 'the door banged and locked forever, I shall have to light a lamp of aggressive voltage in my mind to keep at bay the night.'

I always enjoyed, however, the company of Stephen Graham, who could be relied on to give any young writer the best of advice in words clipped and sibilant. His first book had been written in barrack-room and tent when he was a corporal in the Scots Guards. Just as the great eccentrics have excelled because they had to break the conventional mould of English life, so the guardsman's dreams had to break the iron discipline of the barrack square and the numbing agonies of trench and battle-ground before he could live as poet and writer.

He lived in an old house; not alone, for it was also tenanted by ghosts mostly from the Regency period which Stephen fortunately both liked and admired. So they felt no hostility towards the many guests he would entertain in an all-purpose room with a front door opening into the heart of Soho, and windows looking out on to the prostitutes of Frith Street. Here Stephen would dispense *kvass*, *borscht* and *forshmak*, for he had been on the great Russian peasants' pilgrimages to Russia in the days of 'Holy Russia', and shared their simplicities and mysticisms.

We were often guests, at her country house, of a prolific romantic novelist, Maisie Greig. Maisie, like many popular women novelists, was able to transmute her stories for the transatlantic market merely by changing the names of characters, streets and properties. Katherines became Kays, Herberts became Bretts, Piccadilly, Broadway, and lifts, elevators. The stories varied little. Her husband, Delano Ames, however, wrote excellent detective stories, each with a brand-new plot.

One Saturday morning Stephen suddenly unfurled a white linen banner on which he had boldly painted in red letters, *WELCOME TO DENIS JOHNSTON*. This fine Irish playwright was expected to arrive by train for luncheon. Stephen duly marshalled us at the small wayside station and instructed us how to bear the banner on high, no easy matter when a high wind is blowing from the Wiltshire Downs.

By the time the train arrived, the banner, which stretched

flapping like a giant flag from end to end of the station, obliterated the name so effectively that Denis, immersed in his manuscript of *The Moon and the Yellow River*, was carried on to Reading, where he lunched at a one-star hotel and caught the next train back to London.

I must have been propping up a bar in the neighbourhood when my brother Brian noticed George Bernard Shaw walking ahead of him in Curzon Street. The great man stopped outside the books displayed in our window. Brian at once invited him into the office where he signed the visitors' book, completing his signature with an enormous flourish like the final bars of *Götterdämmerung*; but he shied away from the decanter of Madeira, though he congratulated Brian on a lovely edition of the complete works of Jane Austen we had just issued.

A few months later Brian, who was popular with theatre people, persuaded Sir Cedric Hardwicke to write his autobiography *Let's Pretend*. Hardwicke had played in most of Shaw's plays, both in Malvern, London and New York, and the completed book was remarkably interesting, both as a life story and as a book of the theatre. If Brian was embarrassed when Cedric begged him to ask Shaw to write a foreword to the book, he was even more so when the great dramatist's reply came, written on the usual postcard: 'Dear Brian Grayson, *Cedric is old enough to stand on his own feet.*' Shaw was prolific with his postcards. On a Surrey green I once saw the announcement in large lettering at the foot of the billposter advertising the village fête.

> GEORGE BERNARD SHAW HAS BEEN INVITED BY THE CHAIRMAN AND COMMITTEE TO PRESENT THE PRIZES—HIS USUAL POSTCARD OF REFUSAL WILL BE AUCTIONED AT THE END OF THE DAY.

Brian also commissioned a book from the Duke of Manchester, which ran into many editions. Kim was a man of great charm, a brilliant card player and a 'character'. He was as honest as circumstances allowed, but he was always excellent company, particularly when the decanter was circulating and a certain hard glitter had left his eyes. Through some misunderstanding over the family portraits (which were entailed) it was discovered that the originals had been sold to an American, but not before they had all been copied by a very capable artist; nevertheless those pictures which graced the walls of Kimbolton were still not quite everything they pretended to be.

He had another place in Ireland, an addition to Battlemead, near Maidenhead, where at weekends one could meet the leading theatre and film people with whom he liked to surround himself, particularly if they played poker. In those days a duke was more like a duke than any duke had a right to be, unless he was Bendor Westminster.

From Ireland's 'four green fields' another couple of gifted young writers came to us, Jasper Power and Francis Stuart. Being an old friend Jasper had been around Curzon Street from its beginnings; and I remember his delight when the cigarettes in the waiting-room were stolen on the first day we opened shop; and his even greater delight when, on the second, the silver box containing them also took off. Jasper, alas, suffered from certain compulsions.

Francis Stuart was a mystic, marred by a leprechaun mischief and balanced by an innate protestant shrewdness. He was a convert and hence '*plus catholique que le Pape*' whom he suspected of certain heresies. He wrote for us *Beware of Pity*, a work of great beauty and compassion.

It is always with a sense of pride and gratification that a publisher sparks off the first stars in a writer's career, but often even the suggestion for a book can be very rewarding. Charles Duff was more than an erudite scholar: he was a humane man and a natural writer. He had written a most impressive *Handbook on Hanging*, a masterpiece expressing with wit and clarity the views of civilized man. For us he compiled with ironic skill an *Anthropological Report on a London Suburb*, written in his most charming off-the-cuff manner; but he was able to freeze the facts and summarize statistics with such deadly accuracy, that had it been more widely read by those concerned, it would have caused consternation in the wilds of suburbia; and in the boardrooms of the building societies, great hire-purchase and insurance companies.

The two assembly points for Low Bohemia where we met most frequently were The Plough and The Fitzroy Tavern. A 'literary' police constable of the period, later to be Tom Pocock of the *Evening Standard*, was given this warning by his Superintendent:

'There are two public houses on the sub-division that you are to avoid, The Fitzroy Tavern in Charlotte Street and The Plough near the British Museum. They are used by undesirable characters who call themselves artists, writers or poets, and who are nothing more than wasters. And—er—women passing themselves off as artists' models.' This was a very uncharitable way of describing some of the most distinguished writers, artists, musicians and sculptors of the day.

After The Fitzroy and The Plough had closed, those of us with money (faithfully accompanied by those without) would meet at the Café Royal in the Brasserie to discuss cabbages and kings over long slim glasses of pilsner, seated at the same marble-topped tables and leaning back on the same red-plush banquettes on which Wilde, Aubrey Beardsley and the pre-Raphaelites had lounged and dropped the *bon mot* and fired off the neat retort. Nicol was the original proprietor—hence the Napoleonic N on the silver and plate; he had built and designed the Brasserie for the pleasure and relaxation of people of the night; but by the twenties the gold on the panelled walls had faded and the mirrors mildewed. Caryatids still supported the peeling paint of the ceilings with bored indifference, and plush curtains, guardians of the night, kept out the daylight; but it still retained an atmosphere dignified, decrepit and *fin du siècle*.

Nina Hamnett, who might have been described at that time as Queen of the Non-Establishment, would usually arrive at eleven o'clock; I had been rapidly initiated into her circle, if not into her boudoir. She had a healthy appetite for young men, although she had blossomed beyond the beauty of the dark flower she must once have been: she continued painting until the glass in her hand had become more comforting than the brush.

She was a remarkable woman. Conversationally she could outwit any of us, including Augustus John, and in experience she must have been a hundred years older than most of us. She was born in Tenby, where she first met John through his sister, Gwen John. Nina had been an art student in Paris and had married a Belgian baron—according to the *Almanach de Gotha*. Nina found out that this *mariage à la mode de Gotha* entailed scrubbing the baron's floors, so she decided it was time to leave Paris, which she did directly and discreetly after a successful exhibition of her pictures.

Years later she really fell in love, and as token and proof bought the young lover a motorcycle. The inevitable day came when she surprised him with a young girlfriend on the pillion. A few days later she turned out the light in her studio, turned on the gas oven, and lay down to die; but the shilling in the meter ran untimely out. Waking to life alive she staggered to the bathroom where ineffectually she used a blunt carving knife on her wrists. Her determination to die was like the rape of death itself; she threw herself out of the window. Below, the waiting Victorian spiked railings did the trick in a trice. There are no strict procedures on how to die before your time.

Philip Heseltine—'Peter Warlock'—the brilliant Elizabethan scholar and musician, now chiefly remembered for his *Capriole Suite*, and sturdy champion of Delius, gassed himself in a Chelsea basement. His friend Jack Moeran, who put Joyce's poem to music, stepped off the edge of Kenmare pier when he'd 'drink taken'. The death of Constant Lambert, that talented writer, conductor and composer, though not violent, seemed not unsought. These were hard days for the sensitive and gifted.

It was Nina's brother-in-law, a grandson of General Booth, the great Salvationist, who brought us the news of her death. Augustin Booth, despite his ancestry, was French by birth—he was born to the founder of *L'Armée de Salut*—and in his vocation and attitude to life. He had renounced the fleshpots and security of the Salvation Army to paint and preach the gospel of Cézanne, Manet and all their great sodality, an impecunious and precarious vocation. '*C'était folie de vieille fille*,' he said, shaking his head in sorrow as we raised our glasses to her memory.

Bertie Hollander, a friend of my Riviera days, was one of the regulars at the Café Royal. He was a man of many worlds and many friends. My nephew Ronnie married Babette, the gorgeous daughter of Bertie's brother, Count Hollander. Bertie was a *bon vivant par excellence* and liked to mix his company with his drinks. In London, Cannes and Monte Carlo our similar protean temperaments brought us often together. One was not likely to meet him in the hill towns of the Alpes Maritimes or wandering in the wilderness of wild flowers, sweet-smelling mimosa and orange trees that surrounded them—but one would find him in the smart restaurants, the homely *bistros* and the *bôites de nuit*, often seated alone in the best of all company: a bottle of vintage Nuits St Georges.

He had a pleasantly extravagant friend who disliked handling silver, copper or zinc: the waiters would hopefully bring his change after a dinner party in pyramids of *sous*. But the man was not fooled so easily, and invariably he invited us to recharge our glasses and light up fresh cigars in order to reduce the *pourboire* to a reasonable amount. When Bertie was up at Cambridge he spent so much time racing that his father sent him a telegram: 'Why not take a flat in Newmarket and visit Cambridge occasionally?' Though Bertie was stamped with what the French tax collector terms *signes de la richesse exterieure* he was often very hard up. During one of these lean periods he rather rashly took on a bet for £500 to walk from Paris to Nice. On the night of the 28th with still a few hours in hand he staggered to the Hotel Ruhl exhausted, ragged, down-at-heel and thirsty. Maurice Ruhl immediately put him to bed and summoned the hotel doctor. After examining Bertie the distinguished medico recommended him to drink more red wine (surely an impossibility) and, secondly, that he should take some exercise. Unfortunately Bertie was too weak to throw the good doctor into the courtyard.

Bertie spoke perfect French and I once saw him borrow a taxi driver's cap and go into Maxim's, where he accosted a complete and unsuspecting stranger, demanding an unpaid fare in the latest *argot*. Paul, the head waiter, with his scullions, was in the joke and we were soon seated at the bewildered man's table with a magnum of champagne to placate him.

One evening in the Café Royal, by an unhappy chance, I learned of the isolated world in which certain people must have their being. I had gone to the men's room and suddenly decided, in a jaded and stupid moment, that it might quieten down the party I had just left if I returned in the guise of a clergyman. I reversed my collar and waistcoat so that its black satin lining came to the fore. With the clerical grey suit I was wearing the transformation was complete. On my way back to the Brasserie I became immediately conscious of eyes turning away from me and embarrassment ousting conviviality. Only when it was impossible to avoid my presence were glances, a mixture of guilt and respect, directed towards me, behaviour to which I was quite unused.

When my own rather hilarious party spotted my clerical garb they were encouraged to drink my health in further *steins,* crying: 'Bung-ho Bishop! Cheers Cantuar! Prosit Pope!' Now I felt embarrassed. I was aware of sly glances from the surrounding tables caressing me and disapproving ones stabbing me. I no longer belonged to the world of my own rowdy party, and I was certainly disgracing some good man's calling. What was to have been a harmless joke had gone sour. I was desperately ashamed and slipped away feeling like a chastised cur. I called a taxi and even the driver didn't fail to remind me, 'Careful of the step, sir.'

Sometimes our company would be enriched by musicians: they would usually arrive separately. I never felt there was the same comradeship between musicians and painters as between writers; but it must have existed with Rimsky-Korsakov, Borodin and Mussorgsky. There were, of course, exceptions. Arthur Bliss, a friend of the family, was with me at my preparatory school, Bilton Grange. He studied with Mr Lucas, our music master; or rather this charming organist studied with him because he must have often wondered exactly what was happening when his young pupil, one day to be Master of the Queen's Musick, played notes on the piano and 'cello in his own strange order; but producing lovely sounds and pulling out organ stops in a contradictory combination of harmonies sweet as steel, steely as honey.

Arthur was that rare thing, a man with the soul of an artist and the bank account of a wealthy man, so he helped his fellow composers, orthodox or *avant garde*, by giving special performances of their works. They took place near Paternoster Row, and the cream of the critics and the music publishers would be invited; and even people like myself who just loved music.

But Arthur, like Vaughan Williams (Daddy) and Walton, was at the apex of the musical pyramid. There were others I loved who you might say were painted in water colours rather than oils. A man I liked was Eric Coates. He could have composed more serious music, I suppose, but he was possessed by the spirit of melody, in waltz-time or march-time, and he had a natural gift for graceful pastoral music. He must have earned a fabulous income through the Performing Right Society for broadcasts and recordings, to say nothing of concerts, particularly those in the northern capitals where they loved his music. I believe the BBC eventually paid him a lump sum annually for broadcasting *Music While You Work, Knightsbridge* and his other charming suites. When I put on one of his compositions on the radiogram it always amused us to watch him edging closer and closer to it, until at last he was standing over it conducting with a spoon, a paper knife, my pipe or anything that came to hand as a bâton.

I used to leave the charming company of his wife and family in the flat in Baker Street and go on to Frank Bridge's home off Church Street. He was a delightful companion whose whole life had been devoted to his art; in many ways he was quite unworldly, and like most men with a point of concentration he had shed himself of the superfluous adjuncts of life and left everything in the hands of his devoted wife. Fortunately for later generations his music is played more often as the years grow old.

I can never go into Harrods without laughing and thinking of Peter Warlock as Aldous Huxley depicted him in *Chrome Yellow*—the handsome bearded artist to whose soundproof studio housewives from Wimbledon or somesuch (up for a day's shopping and maybe a little romance) unwarily accepted invitation. Harrod's was his favourite beat, one might say. How, on their return home to suburbia and their industrious husbands, they explained their disinclination to sit down, not to mention lie down, has always intrigued me.

Like Percy Wyndham Lewis, Constant Lambert had been befriended by the Sitwells, whose instinct for recognizing talent was a form of genius. At the time I knew him he was drinking heavily between hours of intensive rehearsing and creative work. We used to meet at The Sun in Splendour at Notting Hill, near where he was living, and it was seated at an old piano, topped with tinkling glasses and splashed with beer, that he first played to me the delicious little phrase as cool and sweet as a mountain stream that eventually flowed into his *Rio Grande*, which he was composing at the time.

He was an impulsive man. For some months he had been madly in love with the Hollywood Chinese star, Anna May Wong, haunting the cinemas where her films were appearing. One day by chance visiting a friend, the door was opened by her Chinese maid, a replica of Anna May Wong herself. Constant, it was said, grasped her by the waist and carried her straightway to a registry office—all his friends knew was that it seemed no time at all before he was married and she was in the family way; but he seemed bent on self-destruction and all her charm and beauty failed to deter him. Proust understood and expressed with force and bitterness the incessant instability of life; only he among the writers I have read expressed so fiercely the continuous uncertainty that makes life a chain of half-experienced deaths.

What was it that made so many of this generation, *hommes fatals*, full of years and talents, so afraid of life and so little afraid of 'nowhere'?

On s'entre—on crie
C'est la vie
On crie—on sort
C'est la mort.

Alastair Crowley, the Black Magician, had propelled his drug-charged body to see us; looking into his yellow eyes, set in a brown-pocked yellow face, across the two-foot-wide Georgian table that divided us, I was truly revolted. The manuscript, the story of his life, ran to about 300,000 words and I promised the book would receive our immediate attention. When he left the room I opened the door and windows to rid the room of the atmosphere of aromatic evil he had left on his brief visit. I have already explained that the rule of the house was that no one bearing a manuscript should be turned away without seeing one of us, and when he had been shown up I had not in fact associated him with the man who liked to be known as the Beast 666. So my first impression of him was in no way influenced by hearsay.

I had met Betty May, the dark-haired artist's model who sat for John and Epstein. She was known as 'the tiger-woman' and like most models had acquired poise and current culture from the artists and writers she had consorted with. In addition she was a delightful folk-singer and first-class cook who had acquired her art the hard way over the studio stove. At the time I met her she was the companion of Edgell Rickward.

Betty, as a girl-bride, had gone to live together with her undergraduate husband, who had fallen under Crowley's influence in the 'monastery' that the Beast had founded on Corfu. She told us that the women members of the mystical community at their periods were constrained to wear a gourd between their thighs to catch the menstrual flow; which from the remotest antiquity has been deemed to possess most powerful magical properties. Dried and pounded to powder, they were a main ingredient in the Host in the Black Mass of which Crowley was the daily celebrant.

It was in her absence from the 'monastery', whose motto was 'Do what thou wilt shall be the whole of the Law' (which has a Rabelaisian ring until one remembers that heroin had replaced wine, the poppy had ousted the grape), that Betty's young husband died his mysterious death.

One version had it that Crowley, celebrating the Black Mass with a hell of a hangover, had slit the throat of his acolyte, Betty's bridegroom, instead of that of the sacrificial goat; who had cut up rough at certain of the sexual activities that were expected of him. Anyway, whatever the truth, there was a terrific scandal and Mussolini was so outraged that he expelled the oblates from the island.

The manuscript Crowley brought us was as strange and sinister a work (unpublished until recently) as one would expect; it was the only book I remember turning down for no better reason than our instant dislike for its author.

Anything can happen in a publisher's office at any time. We should have had *prie-dieux* in every room where, on morning arrival, the directors and staff would devote a few minutes prayer for the sending of a second Tolstoy, Dostoevsky, Voltaire or Proust, for all of whom in welcome Saint Peter had pulled back the gates of Heaven on their hinges. We would have even commissioned a book to be written over seven years, had it smelt even faintly like *Madame Bovary* or *Ulysses*; and we would have sent the junior clerk to sea on the chance of bringing back a *Moby Dick*.

Brian was away staying with Chris Sandeman (the wine merchant) who had collated a delightfully witty book of letters he had exchanged with a woman friend; so Pat and I, holding the fort, happened to be in the office when two young Americans called with a manuscript, which they claimed was the definitive Oscar Wilde biography. They had gone to as many sources as were available, but they had not obtained the approval of Lord

Alfred Douglas; and without Bosie the Wilde story would be Hamlet without the Ghost. I explained the dangers of libel. No publisher on either side of the Atlantic, I believed, would publish without Lord Alfred's sanction. They gave me full authority to deal with the problem in any way I chose.

I knew, of course, it would not be long before Douglas heard of the existence of this manuscript and that he would at once emerge from his tent in full war cry, armed to the teeth with poisoned legal arrows. It took no more than a cursory glance to see that the book (legally) libelled him from stem to stern, as sailors say, but he had to be told. I cabled the news because I'd heard that Douglas, like myself, was a cable-addict. Cables are short, arrive quickly and scream for immediate attention, and always have been my favourite form of communication; even my love cables. The reply from Douglas-in-Hove came before you could say 'Frank Harris'. He would visit Curzon Street the following day. So it came about that Pat and I, fortified with a bottle of champagne, awaited the coming of this legendary figure, this ghostly character in a Victorian melodrama. As the clock struck noon, Pat, who was standing by the window on watch, turned to me and said in his best Holmesian manner, 'Unless I'm very much mistaken, Grayson, I think this is our man.'

I hurried downstairs to receive him and if necessary pay off the cab. My fellow Harrovian friend, Francis Queensbury, his nephew, had told me how he helped him financially; but he had not warned me how charming and disarming his uncle could still be. He was wearing a well-worn suit, well-worn in two senses because he gave it charm and dignity. The traces of former beauty, which at once impressed me, were conveyed in a certain quivering tenderness about the mouth, and a flutter of amusement in the eyes. But his mouth hardened and the eyes gleamed darkly when they detected the first mention of his name in the manuscript. As he bent over reading with the decanter to hand, one wondered how much his mind had been poisoned by the painted past; what exact part had this quiet, distinguished old gentleman played in the tragedy of Oscar Wilde's downfall? Wilde wrote that we kill the things we love. In fact, to be more accurate, we devour the things we love. Wilde was *gourmand* rather than *gourmet* in taste. After the stableboys, bellboys and guardsmen, the 'rough stuff' of the lower orders, it is not difficult to under-

Sir Aubrey Smith, the veteran actor, introduced culture and cricket to Hollywood

James Cagney could play a priest or a gangster equally well

The weekly fishing party with David Niven off Malibu

Shirley Temple could always beat me at noughts and crosses

stand how at his first meeting he fell madly in love, head over heels, arse over tip, with Bosie; and unwittingly put back the clock for the normal acceptance of homosexuality by at least half a century.

After Lord Alfred Douglas, whose sonnets have been compared to the Master's, had left, the empty room was still redolent of his personality: the manuscript lay about in scattered leaves as if an angry wind had swept in from Curzon Street, and the glass like the decanter was empty. The manuscript had not even been discussed. All he had done was to tell me to convey a warning message to the authors—as might his father have done to the hall porter at the Bath Club. What manner of man was this, what manner of man had he been? Of one thing only was I certain: if not 'mad and bad' like his fellow-poet Byron, he had undoubtedly been 'dangerous to know'.

In spite of the fascination of publishing I had a dread of doing the same thing daily, meeting the same people and exchanging similar ideas on similar subjects. I was determined never to lose my intense interest in the inhuman daredevilry of life; my escape hatch was my beloved Paris with its river, *quais* and thirty lovely bridges.

So I spent most of my weekends there. Somehow or other I had persuaded myself I would never fall in love again. This must have been a sure sign of self-disgust for I have always believed that an intelligent man during a lifetime falls continuously in love, though realizing that, but for variations in colour, race and creed, it is always with the same woman. I had loved Mariette so recently that now she was no more than a cat in my mind (a magical cat, of course), crouched in security, basking in the Provençal sun and warming herself at her husband's *grand bourgeois* fireside. She would be the best of all French wives, womanly and wise, of infinite tenderness and understanding, one foot in the *cuisine* and the other in the *chambre à coucher*. But 'the heart must pause to breathe and love itself have rest'; remembrance is only another word for regret.

One evening I strolled round to the Rue Faubourg St Honoré where I had an account with a florist. The shop was divided by a transparent screen, and while I was waiting to be served I noticed a girl seated behind it in the more subdued light. I must describe her in the setting wherein I saw her for the first time, because first impressions sometimes change the course of a life. She was arranging flowers into little posies; unnoticed I was able to watch her, just as an art expert examines a canvas; the table lamp cast its glow on to her face as she bent over her task; her dark eyes were almond-shaped, her nose short and a little tilted, her cheekbones slavonic.

She was wearing a scarlet peasant blouse with full white sleeves and little red embroidered bands at her wrists. On her head she wore the sort of black cap I had seen the girls wear in Georgia. She had pushed it back from her dark hair and it seemed almost in danger of falling off. Points of light were pricking the shadowy background, reflected from broad tropical leaves.

When you send flowers to a girl who works in a flower shop it doesn't take long to get to know her or her family; and I have always had a great respect for flowers as a means of establishing one's identity. Soon she took me to her home. There were several of her family there, all princes and princesses; they ran a night club in Montmartre, and at that time to do this successfully Russians (unless they were grand dukes) had at least to be princes.

I was enchanted. I threw my garlands of affection and admiration at her feet. I took her riding in the Bois, we lunched at La Pérouse, dined at the Tour d'Argent, and we did the simple ordinary things, a day on a *bâteau mouche* on the Seine, or an evening at the Bal Boulier, where James Joyce celebrated after he'd arranged for *Ulysses* to be privately printed by Sylvia Beach.

When I see a painting I particularly like, I have a longing to stand exactly on the spot where the artist had set up his easel; so one day I took her to the Moulin de la Galette where Manet painted his famous picture. I made her sit where the girl in the centre of the canvas sat on the edge of the ballroom floor in her striped blue and white dress, with her little straw hat shading her laughing eyes. At Notre Dame she stood with me before the altar where Henry IV as Henry of Navarre must have stood beside Marguerite de Valois, when on the eve of the Massacre of Saint Bartholomew they were married.

We soon found a little restaurant we liked off the Place de Terne where the impressionists used to meet; walked the streets Renoir had trod; sat in seats where the drunken genius Utrillo and his mother had sat. Our meeting place was no more than a *bistro*, but the *patron* quickly adopted us and kept a bottle of

Montrachet waiting on the ice. In her accustomed seat with her dark head outlined against the off-white of the wall, she looked like an unfinished portrait. But after frequent visits the picture became confident and mature. There was the colour of the light, the colour of eyes and lips, a glint of teeth and steel cutlery, green salad, shining crisp, crusty rolls, a golden wine and white tablecloth; but, alas, I was no artist, and in the Valhalla where walk Renoir and Toulouse-Lautrec, both must have envied my luck.

She was that wonderful character part invented by French women, *une petite amie*, a combination of love and companionship, perfection of person and perception of mind; but, alas, though she was utterly irresistible, she was also utterly unavailable.

One day I asked the *patron* at our restaurant how he kept his cheeses in such perfect condition, particularly Brie (*le roi de fromages*) and Camembert (*la reine*). 'I keep them under my mattresss,' he replied. This happened on one of her lively days and she laughed when I explained patiently that the *patron* was to be commended, for here was a man with respect for the truth, however earthy. As an historic instance of honest purpose and uncomplicated simplicity, I told her the story of Ivan the Terrible, who ordered the Dutch Ambassador's hat to be nailed to his head because, although many yards distant, he had failed to remove it in his presence; and of another occasion at the theatre, when the performance of the villain in the play had been so convincing that His Imperial Majesty ordered him to be beheaded when the curtain fell.

Thus, although frustrated, I was living for my weekends in Paris; in fact life started when Badger, the Pullman steward, brought me my first drink on Friday evening as the train slid out of Victoria Station. Travel has been the occupation of my life; and I was usually unconcerned about my destination. It was enough that I was on my way.

I was infatuated by this Russian girl, this creature of my own invention, linked in a relationship like that of an ill-starred brother and sister, each afraid of his love for the other; we wandered through the great *salons* of the Louvre and stood before where Manet's picture hangs. Here I held her hands for the first time and in another *salon* we read the love-words, steel-engraved, dedicated to an unknown Egyptian queen in 700 B.C.

> 'The sweet one—sweet in love, the sweet one—sweet in love, in the presence of the King, the sweet in love before all men, the beloved before all women, the King's daughter who is sweet in love. Blacker is her hair than the darkness of night, blacker than the berries of the blackberry bush. Harder are her teeth than the flints in the sickle. A wreath of flowers in each of her breasts, close nesting on her arms.'

Our hearts were light for as yet we had no secrets to hide. At that time the sparkling wine had only a short way to travel from Rheims, the brothels and streets were alight with girls; the gigolos (glorified *maquereaux*) could be relied upon to bring a dozen ageing and wealthy Anglo-Americans to finance the evening orgy. She was intensely curious about this weird hidden life, but it was only after much begging and beseeching that I agreed to take her to one of these parties.

I could hardly have been described in those days as being austere; but on the few occasions when I'd been at an orgy I can't say I enjoyed myself, though out of politeness to those present I pretended to do so. There is a limit to spontaneous unloving; nakedness like truth is either very beautiful or very ugly. To anyone reasonably normal it is difficult to assume (naked, in public, with a stranger) even run-of-the-mill sexual postures. To demand of him (or her) demonstrations of skill in variations on the theme is, as Noël Coward used to say, even more 'shame-making'. And, anyhow, he can only be sure he is doing all right if everyone else stops to see what he is up to next.

That evening the party was a comparatively mild one. Unless you are determined to enjoy yourself imbued with a kind of team spirit, it can be unappetising to eat a complete dinner, caviar to strawberries, laid out platterless on the naked nether moiety of a recumbent girl without the aid of cutlery and only the curly locks of a little Arab boy through which to wipe greasy fingers. Nor have I ever enjoyed wine drunk from a loving cup rimmed with pasticcio, seasoned with the sickly taste and smell of miscellaneous lipstick. We remained spectators. Silent, she never moved from my side. We made our excuses and left.

Instead of climbing the hill to her home beyond the Place de la Concorde, to my surprise she told the taxi-man to drive to the flower shop in the Faubourg. I paid him off because she had the key to the place, and as we entered the perfumed darkness I sensed rather than saw a great impatience in all her movements. She was undressing and impatient, unloving hands clutched at my clothing. It was as if I was with a stranger. In the sudden shafts of light from passing traffic I glimpsed that she had half-covered her nakedness with garlands of flowers around her breasts; she pulled me down, roughly whispering lewd endearments in my ear, caressing, biting and scratching me. On the rough fur rug I felt her nails tearing my flesh, as though she were taking her revenge on all her father's Bolshevik enemies by tooth and nail, heaving herself over the bounds of healthy lust into a half-world beyond my understanding, to depths where I could no longer follow. Her inhuman laughter and her tears ran over my face and torn throat and her untamed moaning rippled through my hair. In the ironic way of life, when she was closest to me never had she been further away.

She licked my wounds with slow animal kisses until she lay exhausted in my aching arms. I lit a cigarette and forced it between her blood-stained teeth. For a moment she was still, like someone listening to the wind, then slowly her eyes came back to mine and I knew she had returned from wherever in that turmoil of the flesh she had been lost.

'Take me home, my love,' she whispered. Before I left her she asked me very gently, 'Who will sweep up the broken glass, the broken flowers?' I was like a man in a rudderless boat on the Seine in turbulent flood, with only the poplars to guide me. I had no illusions about what had happened; the legend of the were-wolf is too persistent a one to be ignored.

As I walked down the hill under a starless sky my thoughts passed uneasily over the evening; I had learned more about her than she ever intended me to know. I couldn't put the memory of her lovely dark, unseeing eyes, and her unsheathed teeth, steel-white and dagger-dangerous, out of my mind. As I descended the winding Rue Lepic, clouds covered Paris and there was nothing to warn me of the white full moon riding in the sky.

Next day, after Roberts, the chemist in the Rue de la Paix, had dressed my wounds he looked at me rather curiously and remarked: 'You must keep a young wolf as a pet.' I preferred not to reply.

For the rest of the weekend she was quiet and pensive, paying languid attention to anything I said; and I wondered what dark thoughts were going through her lovely head and I was afraid; we were like strangers in a hotel, together yet distant. During the time I had known her she had been *gamine*, woman, sister, slut and *religieuse*; her moods had been wild and wayward as gossamer: one moment radiant with joy, the next in tears. Her whole being was steeped in superstition. On the weekends following my thoughts were still confused and uneasy. Was what had happened to her an inevitable happening, whose approach she could sense as a shepherd reads the moon and stars? Or was she waiting, minute by minute, hour by hour, day by day, and night by night for the darkness to beckon her again?

We could no longer talk about nothing and enjoy it. Now instinctively I arranged to be with her only in company. There was now, it seemed to me, a permanent soft shadow of disquiet in her dark eyes and a slightly off-balance expression in her lovely face which I had not noticed before. Already I knew in my inner heart that the slow-burning candle of my love was flickering. Once I missed seeing her for a fortnight, then a month, until all light had gone from our companionship. We met no more and so the shadow passed.

I last saw her during the War in Paris where my duties took me. She was walking at nightfall in the Bois de Boulogne, lingering and inviting the attention of those strangers in uniform who haunted the Grande Lac in search of adventure.

There must always be some magic spark remaining in the heart for anyone you have ever loved. There was in mine; but there was also a deadly fear when I saw that there was a full white moon reflected on the waters of the lake.

CHAPTER XI

This warlike, various and tragickal age

ANON

The Edwardian world of my boyhood was gone. Consumed by the fevers of the twenties, its death rattle was only faintly heard as Hitler shrieked and ranted; but at Sutton Park House, my mother's country home, the remaining footmen still wore livery and the butler (last of his line) still ruled paramount over his dwindling staff.

Our old family home in Anglesey, Ravenspoint, once swarming with her children, dependents and retainers, now too huge and full of memories for an old and sometimes lonely woman, was being turned into an hotel by some great consortium. Her numerous sons and daughters, grown to manhood and womanhood, had gone their ways. Her own marriage had broken up—late in life—when one would have thought that whatever difficulties there might have been had long been surmounted.

Mother, wise woman that she was, had been fairly tolerant of Father's 'side jumps' as the Germans call them. When a friend of hers confided that she was praying to Almighty God to put an end to her spouse's infidelities, she told her: 'You shouldn't pray to God. You should pray to the Madonna. You know how these men stick together.'

Mother's technique for dealing with her rivals was to befriend them; especially whenever she found the female installed in one of the many cottages scattered on the estate, there for the use of friends and guests (or let for private profit by the steward). In this way she defused, as it were, many a critical situation; but she met defeat, in the end, from the most unexpected quarter.

One of her greatest friends, whose greatest friend in turn was Princess Beatrice, second daughter of Queen Victoria (surely a solid guarantee of respect for the marital ties) vacated her cottage on the estate for a more commodious life in Father's villa at San Remo. In the past, Father had spent a considerable time at this villa, with its marble floors, lofty ceilings, its tapestries, glittering, glistening chandeliers, curtains of imperial purple framing windows, through which you glimpsed a garden of vivid reds and greens, miniature plantations of marguerites white as starlight among the silver olive trees; and, beyond, the sea that Phillips Oppenheim once described to me as 'blue champagne'.

Father (stout Protestant though he was) was always proud to present the fronds from his palm trees to St Peter's in Rome, the papal blessing for Palm Sunday. He used to board the Blue Train at Victoria and next morning arrive in San Remo, the end of the run, where he could take his time; and where Turner would valet him, not forgetting to change at the frontier the scarlet rosette of the Legion d'Honneur for the scarlet and white of the Crown of Italy, of which order he was a Commendatore. But already the square, syphilitic figure of Mussolini was rising to hasten the end of Father's world.

Now her best friend was queening it amid these splendours. At this Mother devoted herself solely to good works and the numerous family she had raised for him.

When I heard the news, I was astounded to find myself shocked and outraged. I was nearing middle age, estranged from my own wife and entangled in a seemingly never-ending succession of *amours*, and certainly in no position to pass moral judgements; but, as I have said, I was shocked and outraged. The truth is, of course, that we don't expect our parents to share our frailties and imperfections. To the young there is always something obscene in the *amours* of their elders; which has to do with the ambivalence we all display towards the act of love—that whiff of the cloaca always present in our highest and sweetest ecstasies. When Hamlet upbraids his mother he is only voicing disquiet at his own couplings. When Edward VIII, our monarch (and, despite his youthfulness, our father), ran off with Mrs Simpson, outrage was nationwide.

Mother, as I have said, was living at Sutton Park House, the dower house to Sutton Place (then owned by the Duke of Sutherland and now occupied by Paul Getty), the oldest unfortified residence in the country. The house had been added to at different periods; the oldest wing, as old as the garden, dated from Henry VII's reign. A hundred yards away was the little Catholic church where Henry VIII married Anne Boleyn; the vestments of the priest at the royal nuptials were worn by Mother's own chaplain at the Mass, where she prayed for the salvation of us all.

The estate was split by a river curving like a sickle blade through green smooth pasture where sleepy cattle grazed. At the point where the drive crossed the little bridge the water overflowed the banks, and here the land was sewn with rush and sedge and starred with forget-me-not. The plovers cried above the reeds and in the evening the sky was filled with pigeons flapping home to the copses that dotted the park. In the formal garden, within the close-cropped yew hedges, there were roses of every kind, beautiful even when the winter had crystallized them in ice. A great chestnut grew almost too close to the house; had it fallen it seemed that half the county would go with it, and certainly the Dower House. There was an artificial waterfall splashing into a series of pools, and against a sun-warmed wall a huge magnolia spread its blossomed branches like a magnificent candelabra on an altar to gigantic gods.

During the War the house was requisitioned by the War Office for those dear girls in the W.A.A.C. who had heeded the beckoning of Venus rather than the sabre-rattling of Mars. I must say that I never saw more charming and delightful children and rejoiced to see that *l'amour* had not been neglected amid all the ugly blood-letting.

On the Guildford Road entrance, iron gates of interlaced design opened on a pulley system operated from within the Lodge. When a special signal announced an arrival the gates opened silently as if by magic, a constant source of wonder and delight to the grandchildren, who called them 'the fairygates'.

It was a great sprawling mansion of winding corridors on different levels and many rooms, all occupied at weekends when the family arrival with children and dogs and friends and friends of friends. Here Mother reigned supreme, a restless and all-absorbed mother, grandmother, friend, hostess with her rich bohemian way of life, wit and malapropism. She highly approved of Charles Laughton in *The Mutiny on the Bounty*, although she was of opinion that talking pictures were merely a 'flash in the pan' and were not here to stay.

On occasion, when argument ran high, she intervened, and in her forthright way, said, 'If anyone's going to decide the argument it's me, because I'm the top dog in this house.' From then on, though overtly 'Mum' to all of us and to her friends, to the family in secret she was always to be 'Top Dog'.

Ernest Laing was still with us as her private secretary, trying to keep her finances in some sort of order—he had as little success as with his own. He was older, greyer; but his waistcoats were still bright-hued, his handkerchief still scented and his buttonhole still aglow. He did all the household ordering, including the enormous Sunday sirloin of beef which he personally chose. He supervised the chef and manservants. Mother would have no women-servants, other than a sewing maid. Ernest had acquired a dog of his own, which rarely fraternized with our own or the guests, and being a male dachshund he rather unkindly christened it 'Hitler'. He would walk down to the local twice daily; in the morning to put on his bets over a glass of sherry with the landlord; and in the evening to hear how much he'd lost. Hitler always accompanied him.

Once a year, round about Christmas, the whole family, young and old, would meet in her huge London flat in Albert Hall Mansions, from whence, after much champagne or ginger beer, it would proceed in a hired London Transport bus on a tour of the metropolis, whose beauties and oddities would be pointed out to us by my brother Brian. The tour would end at the Olympia Fun Fair in Bertram Mills' Circus, whose swings and roundabouts, coconut-shies and fortune-telling booths and bars would be aswarm with Graysons; until the children began to droop from exhaustion and were whisked home by their nannies and au pairs so that their elders could begin their investigations into the current night-club situation. Frisco, the celebrated coloured gentleman whose night-spots in London and Paris were not exactly resorts for the delicately nurtured, always gave Mother a tremendous welcome on these visits; and saw to it that no 'ruderies' transpired in her presence and the grosser immodesties were purged from the acts of her performers.

It was perhaps from these hilarious but wearying occasions that Father had taken flight, surveying all family proceedings contentedly from afar. Old lions don't mind a gambol with their progeny when they are adorable cubs; but keep well away from them once they are grown. At Sutton Park only the twins were now left with Mother; and spent their time designing and building a huge aviary that may have inspired Lord Snowdon's later structure. I myself had never had any luck with birds.

At this time I had a 60-foot motor yacht which I kept at a yard at Littlehampton, manned in my absence by my pet parrot. News came to me that he had died. He had been found sprawling in the sand of the cage, like the bright body of a stricken matador. I was particularly distressed because he was a good friend. I had nursed him from a tropical Brazilian port into an English winter, a transition made possible only by doping him with whisky at all hours of the day and night; so that for most of the voyage home we both swayed and lurched, irrespective of the movements of the ship. We had become close friends, united in our drinking bouts. He had lived with me and talked to me in drunken sailor language in perfect understanding. I was going to miss him.

I had even less luck with pigeons and peacocks. Years later, in flight from a particularly trying domestic dispute, I found myself exhausted, weary and longing for sleep, crossing the Gibraltar Straits on board the *Mons Calpe*, headed for Tangier, Europe's bolt-hole and Africa's gateway. There, I calculated, in Tangier's elegant squalor, I could take refuge from all social obligation and marital recrimination; and sleep.

I booked a room in a hotel and, without unpacking, went straight to bed—but not, alas, to sleep. A lift, *un ascenseur*, newly installed and obviously the pride and joy of management, staff, visitors and a large chunk of Tangier's populace, was in continuous rattling operation next to my bedchamber. All complaint was useless; there was no other room vacant. I dressed and staggered down to the bar; and solved my problems. A charming American woman, a writer and a chance acquaintance, greeted me, heard of my plight; and at once handed me the keys of her apartment. She was just on the point of taking off for

Paris, would be away for a week and I could go there and sleep for as long as I wished.

I transferred at once, taking only shaving tackle, toothbrush and Bokhara praying rug; and found myself on cool, tiled floors with sunshine-yellow walls, shelves of paperbacks, record-player, stacks of discs and a bed with clean sheets and gaily striped Moroccan blankets; perfect background for a Vassar girl and a haven for the weary.

I unrolled my prayer rug, turned back the covers, stripped naked and opened the door of the bathroom, toothbrush in hand. A maniacal shriek deafened my ears and chilled my blood. The spacious room was already occupied—by a couple of peacocks, man and wife. An instant and instinctive aversion took possession of us, at least of the gorgeous cock and myself, for his drab mate seemed indifferent and *au dessus de la mêlée*. His great fan slowly spread, scintillating and aquiver, as again he shrieked and advanced on me, neck outstretched and beak poised ready for the peck. Instinctively, my left hand *en garde* at fortune's middle parts, my right fencing with the toothbrush, I leapt back into the bedroom. The peacock followed, full of ill will.

Frontal nudity in certain circumstances has its advantages, but this wasn't one of them. I felt as I used to in the trenches when caught by shellfire while squatting in the latrine—exposed and very, very vulnerable. Hastily I began to build a barricade—old suitcases, the sofa, books, boxes, anything—around the bed. I lay there besieged, my moans answering his shrieks, until first light and a chance of escape when the *fatima*—the local char-lady—would appear.

From my non-existent Arabic and her incomprehensible French the pieces of this lunatic mosaic took shape in my exhausted mind. The *mustapha*—the conciérge—reared peacocks to sell to tourists. Knowing Madame was off to Paris and as he himself had urgent business in Agadir, he had installed the peacocks in the empty flat. He would be away for some days, and without his consent and assistance it was impossible to evict the peacocks.

I crawled back to the hotel, out of which I had flounced, as it were, and begged to be taken back. I had no strength left to go elsewhere. My luck seemed about to change. In my absence a room away from the indefatigable *ascenseur* had fallen vacant.

I fell on the bed and prepared for sleep; only to be assailed by a muted roll of thunder, or some seismic disturbance, rising and falling in intensity. *Ku-u-r-pp—Ku-u-r-pp*: a sound of turtle-doves of which I knew at once there could be no surcease. Frantically I rang for assistance and explication.

The rooms about me, I was told, were occupied by a dove-act, Signor and Signora Columba, and their doves, adorable creatures, perched there billing and cooing all the lifelong day until the evening when they fluttered in their cabaret act through tinselled hoops, ringing silver bells. Bone-weary, I accepted Fate's judgement on me and caught the boat back to Europe and domestic strife.

The twins, in addition to their avian activities, were also film-struck, and in their frenzy dragged Mother from cinema to cinema until, as she complained, she didn't know whether she was seeing *Beau Hur* or *Ben Geste*. They had probably caught the affliction from the directors and producers brought down to Sutton by my brother-in-law, Dick Rawlinson, who had switched his attentions from plays to film-scripts. They seemed mostly to hail from Hungary, even when they came from Hollywood.

One of them, Lothar Mendes, a charming and famous director, had taken a great liking for English beer and spent most of his time in the local; and became an object of some curiosity to the rustics. I heard him once being cross-examined by the village gossip, Harry Mather, who used to preface every query by: 'If it isn't a rude question, sir. . . .' He addressed himself to Lothar: 'If it isn't a rude question to ask, I hear as how you make these here cinnymattygraf pictures we sees?'

'I make not all of them.'

'If it isn't a rude question, I reckon you live out there in Hollywood, eh?'

'Why, yes, I do.'

'I suppose as you're married, sir, if it isn't a rude question?'

'I am.'

'Like them others I suppose you've been married pretty often?'

'No, only once.'

'Reckon there's a lot of money in this 'ere fillum business?'

'Lots, and more every day.'

'If it isn't a rude question, sir, you've made a bit in your time, eh?'

'Just a bit.'

'I'd like to ask—if it isn't a rude question—how much d'you reckon you make a week?'

Lothar drank his beer with deliberation, replaced the tankard on the counter, rose to his feet, and eyed his man steadily.

'And I'd like to ask, if it isn't a rude question,' he said gently, 'why you don't mind your own bloody business.'

A roar of laughter went up from the company and there were shouts of 'Good for you, Yank.' Henry was silent and thoughtful for the rest of the session.

Another source of infection was Pat Kirwan, who was himself now writing scripts, an occupation on which he had entered as usual by mistake. He had received a mysterious message asking him to call upon a Mr Alexander Korda (of whom he had never heard) at an office opposite Claridge's. He was received by an imposing man with a thick mane of hair and a heavy central-European accent, who rolled towards him a huge cigar taken from a small coffin over the vast desk, smiled, indicated a lighter, took up a telephone receiver and said: 'Please get me Hollywood. I wish to speak to Marlene.'

Replacing the receiver, he turned to Pat, by now enjoying the truly magnificent cigar (rolled from leaf grown on Korda's own plantation on his own islet in the Caribbean), apologized for the telephone call, and said: 'I wish you to write a feelm about our Indian Army for ze leetle boy Sabu.'

'But I know nothing about films, Mr Korda,' Pat said.

'I know about feelms. You know about soldiers.'

'Why do you think I know about soldiers?'

'Because you have written about Mr Kipling and you know Mr Kipling. If you know Mr Kipling then you know about soldiers.'

In spite of the weirdness of the logic, Korda was right. Pat had been born 'on the strength' and was a youthful but serving soldier when the First World War broke out; and now within days found himself sailing in troopships to India, catching sea-planes to Egypt and re-enacting the 'little wars' of the British Raj with hundreds of Lascar extras and 'ze leetle boy Sabu' up on the North Welsh Frontier of Cader Idris.

Under these influences the twins decided to write, direct and produce films. I myself was calmly going about my business as writer and literary scout, aloof from this frenetic world, when suddenly I had a message from Father who, despite the fact that he had 'gone off' with 'that woman', was still by remote control running our various lives.

Vacant film studios in London were to be bought and equipped; and in the meantime I was to take the twins to Hollywood, where they were to study the technique and tricks of the film business.

Father had, of course, booked us in a suite on the *Mauretania*. In first class we were surrounded by the doddering and wealthy; while in the Tourist Class girls both impecunious and delicious with their watchful boyfriends abounded, who as we smuggled ourselves into their midst greeted us with cries of 'What, slumming again!' In spite of this admirable display of class-loyalty we enjoyed ourselves and shared with them our surfeit of caviar.

Normally the availability of caviar on transatlantic liners is not publicized; it is produced only for the few, not the moneyed few, but the devout. I was immediately marked as one of the faithful. The chief steward will tell you that if they recognize an addict they will forgive your other failings even when you send back the larks' tongues. It was in plentiful supply as none of our fellow First-Classers seemed to like it. I was reminded of our troops sent to Russia to reinstate Kerensky after the First World War, when an officer, inspecting his men's rations (caviar—local produce) as per King's Regulations, asked whether they had any complaints. The reply came back loud and clear: 'Yes, sir, this 'ere jam tastes of fish.'

The best caviar is, without doubt, the Beluga, and my own recipe is the simple one: lemon juice, Cayenne pepper or ahie out of its wooden pod (Mother used to get it from Chile), vodka or well-chilled Chablis; and the company of a beautiful girl of any nationality who likes caviar and has relish for its stimulant effects.

Before travelling on to California I spent a couple of days in New York the ever-changing, which I found more changed than even I expected from the old prohibition-gangster era.

I had been an honorary member of the Knickabocker Club, and it was here I ran into an old friend, Edward, Lord Stanley of Alderley, a pleasure-loving adventurer in the best traditional and honourable sense and a man with a first-class brain. He had already led a full life with a string of beautiful ex-wives in his wake, dripping in mink, chinchilla and sable; and trailing clouds of Dior, Chanel and Guerlain. He was working in New York with the bankers Morgan Grenfell. That evening we played the great dangerous game of 'drifter' (which can lead you into lots of trouble) whose only rule is that you have a good time as directionless you drift. We were challenging New York as Diaghilev, bored, challenged Cocteau: *'Etonne moi, Jean!'* Late in the evening we told our taxi-driver to take us to any place amusing, and we landed up at a sleazy club perched on the top of a steep flight of steps. We ordered a bottle of champagne, though each of us was already as mellow as a harvest moon; and surveying the room Edward quoted Alfred Noyes:

Fat wet bodies go wobbling by
Garbed in satin though God knows why.
Clasped by a satyr in white and black
With a fat wet hand on a fat wet back.

The next moment we were joined by two uninvited metallic blondes. The Californian champagne-type wine was as little to our liking as the two young blondes, so we called for the check. When at last it came it amounted to $100 which, it is only fair to say, included the cover charge. While Edward was querying the bill, I noticed four waiters (tougher in stature and more determined in manner than the average waiter) moving up to our table and closing in on us in an unfriendly manner. I drew Edward's attention to their presence, but all he said was: 'Hell, we can fight our way out of this.' As we wouldn't have had a chance of getting out without between us at least one broken nose, one broken arm and possibly one broken leg, but the certainty of four black eyes, I thought of Falstaff's reflections on valour, decided that I, like him, had none of it and sensibly settled the bill. At the time Edward was disgusted with me; but he relented when I told him I had seen one of the girls gripping a bottle under the table ready to crack him one. The moral of this story is clear; in a clip joint it is wiser to pay up, leave with dignity, but on the way out never fail to step on the head waiter's toe with the full weight of your heel, which you should not forget to turn slowly.

After this moving little incident we repaired to The Royal Box, run by Joe Zelli, whom we had both known in Paris. This charming character had established a *bôite de nuit* in Montmartre, patronized largely by the Anglo-American expatriates. On arrival Joe would conduct his customers to a table, explaining that 'only the Royal Box is good enough for you'.

All should have gone well for Joe, but one evil day he was persuaded by an American syndicate with plenty of dollars to open up The Royal Box in New York, only to discover later that the man behind the venture (masked by his nominées) was Owney Madden, gangster and hoodlum. He had recently rubbed out his rival, Dutch Schulz, whose territory he had taken over; and thus controlled every profit-making club, cat-house, laundry, cleaners and trucking company in Manhattan. He was a hardened killer with the power of life and death held firmly in his podgy hands; I had first met him with Douglas Williams, the New York correspondent of the *Daily Telegraph*, whose business it was to know the famous and the infamous, but whose pleasure it was to know the loveliest showgirls and the most sought-after models of Fifth Avenue.

Owney Madden was watching the oval bar with cold calculating eyes. As usual the animal was clothed in black, as if in perpetual mourning for his countless victims. In his company one had to step carefully: the path he trod was as slippery as walking on crushed beetroot. In his silk-lined room above the club, with its basketful of notched guns in a dark corner, we smoked and drank far into the night: a good cigar's a smoke even if there is a smell of death in the air.

Arrived in Hollywood, we rented a bungalow on the corner of La Cienaga and Sunset; and had I then the money the agent asked for its purchase I would now own one of the most valuable sites in the world; and I would be writing this book in the penthouse at Claridge's or the Meurice, instead of on an old cargo boat bound for Rio.

Strangely, in Hollywood, whose scandals shocked the world, no marriage or divorce had ever taken place, for the good reason that there were no law courts there, just as there was no town hall or railway station; and only one single studio within its limits. It was Greta Garbo who first surprised me by saying: 'I have never made a picture in Hollywood nor have I ever lived in Hollywood; I have made all my pictures in Culver City and I have always lived in Beverly Hills.'

On the 20th Century Fox lot I met with no surprises; but an overwhelming sense of *déjà vu*. I stood in Piccadilly Circus, fed crumbs to the pigeons on the Piazza San Marco in Venice, drank a coffee on the terrace of the old Shepheard's Hotel in Cairo, picked my way through a jungle to an African village, rode in a London hansom, a gondola, and a rickshaw. It was like living in a giant nursery of spoilt children, children who liked dressing up and were beautiful and eager. On the mountainside there was a sign HOLLYWOODLAND in letters seventy-five feet high; and why not? Children like to read big letters. I dined with friends who greeted me with a superb dry martini and later poured a vintage Haut Brion into rabbit stew.

We played tennis at the Westside Club and danced at the Trocadero, fished off Malibu with Nigel Bruce, Merle Oberon and my old friend David Niven; and hooked enormous tunny, bass, tarpon and sometimes an ugly shark. We lunched with the Temples and played noughts and crosses with Shirley, a little girl who could earn £1,000 a week and had two guards to protect her. Shirley always won. There is always something to be said for a town where the melons and oranges are cheaper than spuds in London; while next to me at a party I could hear a world-famous star remark: 'Not only has he broken my heart and wrecked my life, but he's ruined my entire evening!'

We swam and rode with Victor MacLaglen, who owned a private zoo and had scored an Oscar as *The Informer* in Liam O'Flaherty's dark story of betrayal. We shot clay pigeons with Clark Gable; and on one occasion Ginger Rogers tapped out Rupert in morse with the smallest and loveliest feet in Hollywood. Bob Montgomery had a Bentley that ate up the miles between Beverly Hills and the Mexican border, occasionally stopping for large draughts of gasoline; for the car, like most of us, could raise a prodigious thirst in the dry Californian atmosphere. I later dedicated a book to Bob, for he had taught me how to mix the best of all Old Fashioneds*; in turn I gave

*One lump of sugar, two dashes of Angostura bitters, one large measure of Canadian Club whisky. Crush sugar and bitters together, decorate with a twist of lemon peel and a slice of orange, using medium-size tumbler, and stir well—then drink and repeat the dose every ten minutes.

him pieces of advice, 'When a girl says, "I don't know why I'm telling you all this", it's the moment to tip your hat over your eyes, lean back and enjoy a deep sleep. And never eat what you can't see; especially if it's in a restaurant with candles stuck in Chianti bottles.'

Occasionally this stream of make-believe eddied into pools of sanity. Once, at Marion Davies' beach house at Santa Monica, during dinner William Randolph Hearst (the millionaire newspaper proprietor, Marion's protector, sponsor, lover and the original Citizen Kane) turned to Brisbane, his senior writer, who had been ribbing me about the unfunnyness of *Punch*. 'And do you think, Arthur,' he said, 'that the *New Yorker* will still be amusing when it's as old as *Punch*?'

There were occasional liquid evenings with Scott Fitzgerald, who in sad decline was being looked after by Sheila Graham. Later she wrote *Beloved Infidel*, surely one of the most sensitive studies of an artist ever written by a woman who loved. In London I used to play squash with her at Grosvenor House (she even excelled at that), when she was engaged to Lord Donegal, my old friend, writer and linguist.

There were Hugh Walpole (plump and gay) and John Collier (small, blue-eyed and heterosexual), two Englishmen drawing large salaries for doing nothing and not enjoying it. Irving Thalberg, the husband of Norma Shearer and head of Selznick, had a weakness for English writers; he liked to have them around, paid them $1,000 a week, but rarely used either their scripts or stories. He liked them as providing *ambiance* in this cultural slum.

Hugh lived in Laurel Canyon where he had to pay for 'protection', a racket the Mafia imposed with complete impartiality on all the wealthy who lived in lonely districts. He was at that time still 'gay' in both senses of the word, confident that soon he would be the Grand Old Man of English letters; but this was before Somerset Maugham, the writer-assassin, killed him dead in *Cakes and Ale*.

After nine months in Hollywood I had become friends with most of these fantastic creatures the world idolized, but who knew nothing of them except for the 'scandals' and 'romances' concocted and released by the studio publicity. I had seen them as human beings, children it is true, but as children acting out their private fantasies and not the commercial celluloid dreams their masters and the world public paid them for. I decided to make a film of them as I knew them, with their hair down *en pantoufles*. Without realizing it I was on my way to becoming the first candid cameraman.

There is, however, a clause in every film star's contract forbidding him (and especially her) to appear before any camera not owned by their own studios. In spite of this, all I approached agreed to do a 'bit'; so I engaged a first-class Swedish cameraman and went to work. Most of the shots were taken at their homes: then to my great surprise I was given permission to take our camera into the 20th Century Fox lot, where I was able to get many amusing shots of the stars in their dressing-rooms, on the sets, even at sessions of films they were making.

Everything seemed to be going along smoothly when, to my consternation, I heard through the jungle telegraph and the radio *trottoir* that the studios had convened a secret meeting at which it had been decided I should not be allowed to leave the state with my negative. I had already learned the ruthlessness and gangsterism that operated beneath the smooth surface of studio life. Very few of the top executives moved about without their bodyguard. Even at Hearst's parties no one could approach him without his nod of approval to the strong-arm men who surrounded him; and the *faux-bonhommes* of the top film echelons were similarly guarded. I knew, therefore, they would have no hesitation in forcing their way into the bungalow, beating me up and stealing my negative—nor could I trust it to any bank whose branch might be dependent on a studio. The issue was finally resolved in a delightful manner—it might almost be said by remote control.

We had come out with very grand letters of introduction from Sir Phillip Sassoon to Mary Pickford; from the Duke of Sutherland to Charlie Chaplin, and so forth; but we also had one from our parish priest, Father Breen, to his brother Joe—and it was this letter that turned the scales because Joe Breen happened to be head of the Hays Office; and the Hays Office had an agreement with all the studios that the last word in censorship rested with them. Consequently none dared offend them. So when the word went out that I was not to be interfered with in any way, and the word was Joe Breen, I was given a *laissez-passer* none dared question.

We came back to London (where Father in the meantime had bought Hammersmith Studios), cut and put a sound track to my film and obtained the best possible distribution terms as an independent producer. I had made what was at that time a unique film, a peep behind the scenes, the first of the intimate sneak-shot pictures, a sort of respectable 'what the butler saw'. At the end of two years I was allowed by the distributors to break financially even.

I soon settled back into my old way of life, a delightful sort of literary vagabondage with none of the discomforts and anxieties of being a tramp. While I had been away my agents had sold the cheap rights of my *Gun Cotton* books to Newnes, so I had money to spend, always a satisfactory position to be in and one which assures you of constant company and fresh contacts.

Grayson and Grayson were doing as well as any small publisher had a right to expect, considering we had neither an extensive sales organization nor a well-established educational line, nor vast resources. Brian had astutely arranged for Commander ('When I was in Patagonia') Campbell to visit the bookshops and bookstalls, where he called attention to our publications, organized displays and saw that our authors' books were at the top of the pile. Campbell was enormously popular as a radio personality, and as a personality in his own right; and he spread the Grayson gospel of goodwill and good books wherever he went. Incidentally, he was a man with the oddest allergy I have ever heard of: if he ate marmalade pudding his head steamed.

Slowly we were compiling a list of new writers to be supported by the old guard, two teams of which we could be proud; we could only hope they would be proud of us. Then one night a strange event occurred, something which happens, or should happen, at least once in the life of every publisher's scout.

I was dining at Richard Hogg's home in Draycott Gardens with his mother and father. The decanter of port was on its third voyage round the table when Mr Hogg addressed me in a gentle voice; but quietly as he'd spoken, his words hit me broadside on.

'We have in our possession,' he said, 'over 150 unpublished letters exchanged between Percy Bysshe Shelley, Mary Godwin Shelley and my ancestor Thomas Jefferson Hogg. Subject to certain conditions you may have the rights to publish them.' In one fortunate evening I had struck gold of the highest quality.

After deliberation it was decided to invite Professor George Gordon to edit the letters. This distinguished and lovable man was President of Magdalen College, Oxford, and Vice-President of the University; and had been Pat Kirwan's company commander in the War. Permission was granted to remove the letters from Mr Hogg's bank to the Bodleian in Oxford. Here transcriptions were made and the originals returned to the Hogg family. Arrangements were made with Random House in New York for simultaneous publication.

In the meantime the world international situation was deteriorating rapidly and breaking up like the final throes of the Ice Age. The Huns were once more on the move: there were other and more immediate jobs to be undertaken by all of us. The inevitable day came when the firm finalized its finances, and the great black Georgian door opened and closed for the last time.

War was declared, and at once it swept us each in our own way into its vortex; the great Shelley venture, which was to have crowned our publishing year and about which we'd all dreamed, gave place to the nightmare of the greater adventure. Three months later we ceased to exist as a publishing house.

As soon as war was declared I reported to the Irish Guards regimental orderly-room at Buckingham Gate.

The wild geese are flighting head to the storm
As they've faced it before.

But they'd no use for this 'undomesticatable' goose who'd been blown up in the 1914–18 War, buried in an adjacent shell-hole and who suffered from a G.S. leg wound. I was informed I would not be accepted for 'normal' (is there such a thing?) soldiering but they might place me with a reserve battalion. I guessed this would mean training young officers, giving lectures I couldn't compose and lessons in the art of killing I couldn't impart; and, to break the monotony, port and biscuits in the anteroom, unless the Bath Olivers ran out. The prospect was dismal. Sydney Fitzgerald, that most charming and humane of men (and Lieutenant-Colonel of the Regiment) wouldn't even rate me as good cannon-fodder, so I retired to my yacht at Little-